LA COUR DE JUSTICE DES COMMUNAUTES EUROPEENNES ET LES ETATS MEMBRES

---

* au 25 janvier 1980

INSTITUT D'ETUDES EUROPEENNES
UNIVERSITE LIBRE DE BRUXELLES

THESES ET TRAVAUX JURIDIQUES

LA COUR DE JUSTICE DES COMMUNAUTES EUROPEENNES ET LES ETATS MEMBRES

Journée d'études organisée
par l'Association belge pour le droit européen
et l'Institut d'Etudes européennes de l'Université libre de Bruxelles

Bruxelles, 25 janvier 1980

1981
EDITIONS DE L'UNIVERSITE DE BRUXELLES

La publication des actes de la journée d'études a pu être réalisée grâce aux subsides versés par le Fonds national de la recherche scientifique et par l'Association belge pour le droit européen.

I.S.B.N. 2-8004-0736-0

D/1981/0171/8

Imprimé en Belgique

PROGRAMME

MATIN

Président de séance :

M. L. GOFFIN
Professeur à l'Université catholique de Louvain,
Ancien président de la Fédération internationale pour le droit européen.

Allocution d'ouverture

M. Michel WAELBROECK,

Professeur à la Faculté de droit de l'Université de Bruxelles,
Président de l'Association belge pour le droit européen.

The Member States, the Judges and the Procedure

Mr. Francis JACOBS,

Professor at the University of London, King's College

Discussion

Les Etats membres et les compétences de la Cour

M. Robert KOVAR,

Professeur à la Faculté de droit et des sciences politiques de Strasbourg,
Directeur des Etudes juridiques au Collège d'Europe de Bruges.

Discussion

APRES-MIDI

Président de séance :

M. Paul-François RYZIGER

Avocat au Conseil d'Etat et à la Cour de Cassation de France,
Secrétaire général de l'Association des Juristes européens.

Les Etats membres et la jurisprudence de la Cour

MM. Jean-Victor LOUIS, Georges VANDERSANDEN et
Michel WAELBROECK,
Professeurs à l'Université libre de Bruxelles.

Discussion

Conclusions de la journée

M. Christian TOMUSCHAT,

Professeur à l'Université de Bonn.

Allocution de clôture

† M. Paul FORIERS,

Professeur à l'Université libre de Bruxelles,
Président de l'Institut d'Etudes européennes.

ALLOCUTION D'OUVERTURE

par

Michel WAELBROECK,

Professeur à la Faculté de droit de l'Université libre de Bruxelles,
Président de l'Association belge pour le droit européen.

Jusqu'il y a peu, l'action de la Cour dans le développement du droit communautaire faisait l'objet d'un consensus général. Certains s'émerveillaient de la hardiesse avec laquelle la Cour élaborait et réussissait à imposer le respect de concepts nouveaux, tels que l'effet direct et la primauté du droit communautaire, et élargissait le champ d'application du traité en donnant une interprétation extensive à des notions telles que celle de « travailleur », de « taxe d'effet équivalent », de « mesure d'effet équivalent »...

Certes, d'autres étaient plus réticents. Toutefois, leurs objections s'exprimaient avec modération.

Depuis quelques années, le ton a changé. Les réserves se sont faites protestations ; des initiatives parlementaires ont été prises pour déclarer sans effet sur le territoire national les délibérations de la Cour ; des critiques sont exprimées ouvertement par les milieux judiciaires et politiques de certains Etats membres, et on assiste même, pour la première fois, au spectacle inquiétant d'un Etat qui, condamné pour manquement à ses obligations, refuse obstinément de s'incliner.

Quelles sont les causes de ce changement d'attitude ? Dans quelle mesure s'explique-t-il par une réaction compréhensible des milieux nationaux à un certain « triomphalisme » communautaire ? Doit-on s'attendre à un infléchissement de la jurisprudence de la Cour ?

Telles sont certaines des questions auxquelles nous avons pensé que ce colloque pourrait apporter des éléments de solution.

Vous êtes venus nombreux pour participer à nos travaux. Je suis très heureux de pouvoir accueillir aujourd'hui les magistrats, professeurs, avocats, fonctionnaires nationaux et européens, juristes d'entreprises, étudiants et chercheurs qui, par leur présence, prouvent l'intérêt qu'ils prennent à l'important débat qui va s'amorcer dans quelques instants.

Je suis particulièrement heureux de pouvoir saluer ici deux membres de la Cour elle-même, Messieurs les Juges Mertens de Wilmars et Pescatore, de même que Monsieur Ehlermann, directeur général du Service juridique de la Commission, et Messieurs Dewost et Glaesner, directeurs généraux au Service juridique du Conseil.

THE MEMBER STATES, THE JUDGES AND THE PROCEDURE

by

Francis G. JACOBS,
Professor at the University of London, King's College.

WRITTEN OUTLINE

I. THE MEMBER STATES AND THE JUDGES

Mode of appointment

Judges and Advocates-General are appointed "by common accord of the Governments of the Member States" (Article 167 of the EEC Treaty). In practice there has been one Judge from each Member State (with an additional Judge when, before 1973, there was an even number of Member States). It could be argued that the Judges should be representative of the legal systems of the Community: at present, for example, there is a representative of the Scottish but not of the English legal system.

Question 1: Should Judges be appointed from "law districts" rather than from Member States?

Question 2: Should the number of Judges be increased?

Term of appointment

Judges and Advocates-General are appointed for a term of six years, which is renewable (Article 167 of the EEC Treaty).

Question 3: Is the present system fully compatible with the principle of judicial independence? Or should Judges and Advocates-General be appointed for a non-renewable (perhaps longer) term, or for life (with provision for age of retirement)?

Question 4: Would it be desirable, especially if judicial appointments were no longer subject to renewal by decision of the Member States, to introduce individual and dissenting opinions?

II. THE MEMBER STATES AND THE COMPOSITION OF THE COURT

Before 1974 the general rule was that all cases had to be heard by the plenary Court. The sole exception, numerically quite important, was for staff cases. Article 95 (1) of the Rules of Procedure, as amended in 1974, allowed a reference for a preliminary ruling to be assigned to a Chamber if it was of an essentially technical nature or concerned matters for which there was already an established body of case law. That exception proved in practice to be very limited, and almost all cases other than staff cases continued to be heard by the full Court.

After the substantial recent increase in the Court's case-load Article 95 (1) was amended with effect from 6 October 1979 to permit the Court to assign to a Chamber any reference for a preliminary ruling and any action instituted by a natural or legal person insofar as the difficulty or importance of the case or particular circumstances are not such as to require that the Court decide it in plenary session. A case may not be assigned to a Chamber if trial by the full Court is requested by a Member State or a Community institution taking part in the proceedings, whether as a party, or as intervener in a direct action, or by submitting written observations on a reference for a preliminary ruling. Unless such requests prove to be frequent, the result in practice may well be that, in future, assignment to a Chamber will be the normal mode of trial, and trial by the full Court the exception. The Court has now been re-constituted as three Chambers of three Judges, instead of two Chambers of four Judges.

As a consequence of the recent amendments, it may frequently happen that a Judge from the Member State concerned will not be sitting when a case is heard : not in cases brought by or against a Member State, which will continue to be heard by the full Court, but in direct actions brought by a natural or legal person from a Member State, and references from a court or tribunal of the Member State for a preliminary ruling.

Question 5: Is the new balance between cases heard by the full Court and cases heard by a Chamber satisfactory?

Question 6: Is a Chamber of three Judges too small for the standard case? And in particular, too small to be representative of the different legal systems within the Community?

Question 7: Should the "Judge of the State" sit?

Question 8: Should the German principle of "the legal judge" be adopted or should the composition of the Chambers be flexible?

III. THE MEMBER STATES AND THE PROCEDURE

There seem to be no special problems about the position of Member States as parties in proceedings before the Court where they appear as plaintiffs or as defendants in direct actions. But there have been suggestions that the position of Member States when intervening in direct actions, or when submitting observations on a reference for preliminary rulings, should be improved. In both types of case the Member States have an unlimited right to take part in the proceedings. But in references for preliminary rulings it was said that, because national courts do not always clearly formulate their questions, the Member States may find it difficult to decide whether they should submit observations and, if so, on what issues; that the time limit of two months was too short; and that there should be an opportunity to reply in writing to the written submissions of others. In direct actions, it was said that Member States should have access to the pleadings in order to be able to decide whether to intervene and on what issues; and that they should not be required to support either of the parties. The difficulty with access to the pleadings is to reconcile the interest of the Member States with the need to protect the interests of the parties, especially in cases where confidential information might be disclosed. The solution adopted under the new Rules is for the Court to transmit to the Council copies of the Application and of the Defence, but not the annexes thereto, in all cases to which the Council is not a party; in this way, presumably, those pleadings will be available to interested Member States, while confidential information can be put into annexes.

At the same time as the opportunity for Member States to intervene has been increased, the right of the parties to reply in writing to an intervention has been abolished. It appears that, under the revised Rules, a reply to an intervention can no longer be made in writing, but only at the oral hearing.

The abolition of the right to reply in writing to an intervention raises issues of some importance. It may in some cases seriously prejudice a party since an intervention may raise new issues.

This in turn raises the question whether the present procedure for amending the Court's Rules of Procedure is satisfactory. What appears to be lacking is any machinery for consultation with practitioners before changes in the Rules are adopted. Comments on the Court's proposals may be made by Member States in the Council, whose unanimous approval is required for amendments to the Rules. But the Council's proceedings are veiled in secrecy, while justice is a public virtue. Some formal and open procedure for consultation may be necessary, if justice is to be seen to be done.

References for preliminary rulings

Question 9: Can any procedure be adopted to clarify the issues arising on a reference?

Question 10: Is the two months time limit too short?

Question 11: Should there be an opportunity to reply in writing to the written observations?

Direct actions

Question 12: Should there be a right to reply in writing to an intervention?

Question 13: Should Member States have access to the pleadings?

Amendments to the Rules of Procedure

Question 14: Should amendments require the unanimous approval of the Council?

Question 15: Should there be some machinery for consultation with practitioners on proposed amendments?

ORAL REMARKS

INTRODUCTION

In my written outline (1) I have suggested fifteen questions for discussion and have been asked to introduce the discussion in twenty minutes. If I tried to say something about each question, that would leave one minute and twenty seconds for each one. However, I propose to adopt a less mechanical approach and also to start with a general remark, which I think is relevant to many of the questions.

A distinction is sometimes made between the "representative" character of international organisations and the integrationist or supranational character of the Community. Such labels are I think intrinsically dangerous

(1) *Supra*, p. 11.

and misleading, but in some respects I would say that the Court of Justice is, or ought to be, a representative court. That does not mean that the Judges ought to represent the political views of governments, and of course there is no place in the European Court for a judge like some in other international courts, spokesmen for the national interest ; but it does mean that they should represent the legal backgrounds from which they come, and that the Court itself should embody the variety of legal and political cultures which make up the Community. Indeed it might be said that only in this way can the process of legal integration be a genuine process.

I. THE MEMBER STATES AND THE JUDGES

If that is right, then objection cannot be taken to the Treaty provision whereby Judges and Advocates-General are appointed by common accord of the Governments of the Member States. I think that is preferable to, for example, the idea that members of the Court should be elected by the European Parliament from a list of Community lawyers drawn up by the Commission! It is also essential that the Members of the Court should enjoy the utmost confidence of the legal professions in their own countries.

Similarly, I do not myself find anything objectionable in the practice which has resulted in the appointment of one Judge from each Member State. This practice, which is not laid down by the Treaties, has not made the Court an inter-state court. The fact that Judges are drawn from the Member States is justifiable, not on political, but on legal grounds, since Community law is itself based on the legal systems of the Member States. Although therefore the impending enlargement of the Community may seem to risk making the Court too large for practical convenience, at least when sitting as a plenary Court, it seems essential that there should continue to be a Judge from each Member State.

But if the Judges are to be representative of the legal systems of the Member States, the United Kingdom is in a special position in having two separate legal systems, the English and the Scottish — not to mention Northern Ireland, the Isle of Man and other variants. But the United Kingdom has one Judge — at present, a Scottish Judge.

So should Judges be appointed from law districts rather than from Member States — which would also underline the Community, rather than inter-state, character of the Court. That might be a desirable solution if, in fact, the law districts and the Member States were not by and large co-extensive. It might then be possible, for example, to appoint one Judge from two states whose legal systems were sufficiently similar. But this is not in fact, I think, the case, and even if it were, it would be difficult for lawyers to admit it. Thus English law and Irish law have a common basis and many similarities; but an English lawyer will certainly consider that the absence of a representative of the English legal system is not fully remedied by the presence of an Irish Judge; and an Irish lawyer, I think, would take the converse view. Perhaps one answer would be to continue to appoint Judges from the Member States, but to recognise the special position of the United Kingdom by appointing an English and a Scottish Judge: not too shocking a concession, perhaps, since the Court operated until 1973 with two Italian Judges, in order to provide an uneven number.

As to whether the number of Judges should otherwise be increased, that question I would suggest should be answered in the negative. Subject to the need to appoint a Judge from each Member State, and any expansion of the Court resulting from the enlargement of the Community, there are overwhelming advantages in a relatively small homogeneous Court, especially advantages for the continuity and concentration of its jurisprudence. If an increase in the Court's case-load should make it difficult for the Court to function in this way, then almost any reform (2) in its procedures, working methods, or even the scope of its jurisdiction would be preferable to enlarging, and so in a sense diluting, the Court itself. On the other hand these considerations do not apply in the same way to the Advocates General, and here an increase in their number to take account of the pressure of work seems urgently necessary.

Next, is the appointment of Judges for a renewable term of six years fully compatible with the principle of judicial independence? Clearly it is not. More difficult is the related question whether the requirement of a single collegiate judgment should be abandoned and individual and dissenting opinions introduced. I am sure it is sufficiently obvious why these questions are related. It is significant that, some years ago, the judges of the Federal Constitutional Court in Germany were enabled to give individual opinions at the same time as their period of office was extended to a longer but non-renewable term. Should be same be done in the European Court? It is not difficult to point to relevant differences between the Federal Constitutional Court and the European Court. Above all there is the factor which I have mentioned already, that the task of the European Court is to forge a common jurisprudence from the variety of legal systems of the Member States; and the great risk, if individual opinions were introduced, would be the disintegration of that jurisprudence. A second factor is that the authority of judgments of the European Court is still relatively fragile, and there is a

(2) Much has recently been done to this end, e.g., creation of a third chamber, greater use of chambers, appointment of a second Legal Secretary, to assist the Judges.

risk that its judgments would carry less authority if they were not presented as the collective wisdom of the whole Court. A Member State reluctant to comply with a judgment might seek to justify its defiance, however irrationally, by pointing to a powerful dissenting opinion. And the possibility cannot even be excluded, as certain recent cases in the European Court of Human Rights have regrettably shown, that a judge might take advantage of his liberty to express an individual opinion and go beyond the legitimate freedom to differ in order to attack the view of the majority of the Court and undermine the authority of its judgments.

If in the future individual opinions were to become possible, lawyers in the United Kingdom would be the first to welcome such a reform, accustomed as they are to the idea that a judgment is essentially what a particular judge in his conscience believes, and finding the requirement that a judge signs a judgment in which he does not believe scarcely compatible with the concept of judicial integrity — although it must be said that the most eminent English judges served happily for many years on the Judicial Committee of the Privy Council at a time when that tribunal acted by a single opinion. Apart from those insular considerations, the collective judgment of the European Court has other disadvantages which are recognised on all sides, especially by those who have to interpret the more obscure pronouncements which are the product of judicial compromise. A majority judgment in such cases would make for greater clarity, while dissenting opinions might stimulate the development of the law. But those considerations are outweighed, I think, by the need for the Court to speak with a single authoritative voice — a need which is no less now than it has been in the past. Both the advocates and the opponents of the general trends of the Court's jurisprudence would perhaps agree on one thing, that the authority of the Court's judgment is a necessary condition of observance of the law, and so of the Community itself. They would also perhaps agree on the related need for the consistency of the Court's jurisprudence. Consequently, if regretfully, I would dissent from the idea of dissenting opinions.

II. THE MEMBER STATES AND THE COMPOSITION OF THE COURT

Part II of my topic concerns the Member States and the composition of the Court. The new Rules of Procedure enlarging the jurisdiction of the Chambers give Member States two privileges: cases brought by or against Member States will continue to be heard by the full Court; and in other cases, any Member State taking part in the proceedings, or a Community institution, may request trial by the full Court. In those cases however, unless such requests prove frequent, trial by a Chamber of three Judges seems likely to become the norm, and the question I would like to raise is whether such a Chamber is too small for what might be called the standard case.

Certainly an increase in the jurisdiction of the Chambers was necessary to lighten the burden of the Judges. Perhaps too the full Court of nine or more Judges is in any event too large for convenience. But is a division of three Judges not too small?

Is it not too small, perhaps, to command the complete confidence of litigants, and also, most relevant to us today, of Member States, especially in a decision which is final and not subject to appeal. Most cases decided by the Court are cases of considerable importance. As is well known, even cases referred from the lowest courts of the Member States often raise issues of considerable legal, economic, political, even constitutional significance. Is a Chamber of three Judges, which has previously been considered appropriate only for staff cases, or, since 1974, for cases concerning such technical questions as those arising under the Common Customs Tariff, now the appropriate forum for the standard case? I would suggest that a Chamber of three Judges is hardly consistent with the importance of the Court's role, or with the authority which its decisions must carry.

I would add two further comments. First, to have Judges from only three of the Member States conflicts with what I have described as the representative character of the Court. Secondly, and related to that, is a point which is central to our subject today: the fewer Judges sitting, the smaller is the chance that there will be a Judge from the State directly concerned: for example, a Judge of the State from whose court the case was referred. It would be a retrograde step to require, in contrast to the present position, that the Chamber should include the Judge from the State concerned. That might be misconstrued as the appointment of a representative of the national interest. Yet it is widely recognised that it is useful to have sitting in a case a Judge from the country concerned, because he is likely to have a better understanding of the context and background of the case, and of the national law, than Judges from other countries. This was not generally a problem when almost all cases of significance were heard by the plenary Court; but it will be a general problem if it becomes the normal practice for a case to be heard by a Chamber of three Judges.

These difficulties could be partly remedied — but only partly — if the Chambers were somewhat larger; a Court of five judges is sometimes regarded as the best compromise. There is of course another difficulty, of a practical kind, in having two divisions of five Judges sitting at the same time when there are only nine Judges in all; even Solomon did not suggest that a judge could be divided in two. But that difficulty could be overcome by a very small increase in the number of judges, which will in any event be necessary on the enlargement of the Community.

Once again, the advantages of a smaller Chamber must be recognised. It should make it possible for all the Judges sitting to have a closer familiarity with the case. On a pratical level, it reduces the difficulties caused by the need for interpretation of the Court proceedings. It increases the possibility of dialogue between Judge and Counsel, a development which can only be welcomed, especially by lawyers from the United Kingdom, who find it hard even to recognise as judicial a process whereby the Judges listen, however politely, to the argument and then proceed to deliver a judgment which bears little relation to it. English lawyers are accustomed to a very different decision-making process in which the decision is the product of dialogue and of argument, not, as it sometimes appears in Luxembourg, an *ex-cathedra* pronouncement. I have been struck by the greater amount of question-and-answer in cases heard by three Judges rather than nine. But even so, these advantages do not seem to me to outweigh the difficulties I have mentioned. Consequently, I would favour a larger Chamber, perhaps of five Judges, for the standard case, with the smaller Chamber of three continuing to hear cases of limited technical interest, and cases of particular importance being heard by the plenary Court.

III. THE MEMBER STATES AND THE PROCEDURE

Turning now to the Member States and the procedure of the Court, I would like to concentrate here on proposals for modifying the procedure, which raise a fundamental issue about the position of Member States in cases where they are not parties to the proceedings. The questions arise particularly in preliminary rulings under Article 177 of the EEC Treaty where the Member States, without being parties, often have a direct interest in the case, and where although they have the right to submit observations, the unusual nature of the proceedings makes it difficult for them to participate as effectively as they might wish. A convenient starting-point is the memorandum of the United Kingdom Government reported in the *Common Market Law Review* last year, which made a number of suggestions for the organisation of the Court. In particular, the Government made four suggestions designed to enable Member States to be more closely involved in the Court's proceedings. Three of the suggestions concerned references for preliminary rulings under Article 177. They were summarised in an editorial in the *Common Market Law Review* (3) as follows:

1. In the case of references under Article 177 the period of two months which is granted to Member States to make their observations should be extended. This period is too short for the necessary legal research and consultation between government departments.

2. National courts do not always clearly formulate their questions when they request preliminary rulings. Therefore Member States may find it difficult to decide whether they should submit observations and, if so, on what issues. It would therefore be helpful if the Court of Justice would identify the real issues for decision at an early stage of the proceedings, preferably before the opportunity for written observations is closed and certainly before the oral stage.

3. In preliminary proceedings the parties and the Member States have insufficient opportunity to contest each other's arguments. Before the Court of Justice the written, rather than the oral proceedings carry the greater weight, partly because of translation problems in the oral proceedings, partly because of the tradition of the Court. As all the written comments must be presented at the same time, the Member States have no opportunity to meet in their written submissions the arguments advanced by the parties, the Commission or by other Member States. Such an opportunity should be granted.

These suggestions, in the context of other proposals made at the same time, were seen in some quarters as evidence of an attack on the supranational character of the Community. The British proposals, it was said, "breathe the spirit of a close linkage between the Community and the national governments. In such a community the national authorities should be heard as much as possible and should play a maximum role, also in Court proceedings". (4)

But, whatever the political motivation may have been, the procedural problems must be examined on their merits. These problems have their root, in my view, in the limited and inadequate role played by the oral hearing in the present procedure. This is particularly apparent in preliminary rulings, where the observations of the parties, of the Commission and perhaps of the Council and of several Member States, have all been submitted at the same time and where no one preparing for the oral hearing

(3) 1979, p. 3.
(4) *Op. cit.*, p. 5.

knows which of all the issues raised are of real interest to the Court: in preparing for the hearing, the lawyers can only guess, and even at the hearing itself, they will probably not discover the answer.

I would suggest that it would resolve many of the difficulties if the Court, at the end of the written procedure — and this could apply to direct actions also — were to have a preliminary exchange of views sufficient to enable it to indicate in advance the issues on which it would particularly welcome oral argument — and also, perhaps, the issues on which it would not. This would make it unnecessary to expand or extend the written procedure; it would give those taking part in the oral hearing guidance which is at present often entirely lacking; and it would to some extent make up for the absence of dialogue between Judges and Counsel. Far from extending the oral hearing, it might actually save time. It would meet the preoccupations of not only the Member States, but also the parties, and, particularly if the Court were to explain in its judgments its reasons for rejecting the submissions of the parties on the relevant issues, it would come closer to satisfying the curiosity of the losing litigant, who, at least in the United Kingdom, likes to know, if he loses, not only that he has been given the opportunity of presenting his case, but also, perhaps perversely, why he has lost: why his submissions have been rejected. It would be much easier for the Court to explain its reasoning to this effect, if the argument were directed to the issues which the Court sees as relevant. Finally, if the oral hearing were given a greater direction, in this way, the Court's procedure would combine the better qualities of the legal systems of the Member States. Lawyers from the United Kingdom who have experienced the written procedure used in the Court have come to recognise its advantages, at least where the questions at issue are questions of law rather than of fact. But this does not mean that the oral hearing should be a formality. A modest reform might enable both Member States, and the parties, to make a more effective use of the oral hearing, not only for their own satisfaction, but also for the assistance of the Court.

CONCLUSION

Finally, in conclusion, I hope that these introductory remarks have served two purposes: first to point to certain fundamental principles underlying the rather technical questions which are in issue: especially, I would suggest the representative character of the Court, the need for cohesion and consistency in its jurisprudence, and above all the adoption of procedures which will inspire confidence in its work and maintain the legitimacy and authority of its decisions. Secondly, I hope that my remarks have been sufficiently controversial to generate discussion.

DISCUSSION

M. GOFFIN, *président*

Je remercie beaucoup le professeur Jacobs pour son exposé très clair, très concis, mais aussi très anglo-saxon. Aussi est-il probable que certains participants à cette journée d'études ne partagent pas ses vues à tous égards.

Si vous le voulez bien, nous allons grouper les questions en trois catégories :

— le statut des juges ;

— la composition des chambres ;

— la réforme de la procédure devant la Cour.

I. LE STATUT DES JUGES

M. GOFFIN, *président*

Le professeur Jacobs a posé un certain nombre de questions. Pour tenir compte de ce que le Royaume-Uni connaît plusieurs systèmes juridiques, le professeur Jacobs a proposé — si j'ai bien compris — qu'il y ait trois juges britanniques alors qu'il n'y aurait qu'un seul juge pour chaque autre Etat membre.

D'autre part, il estime que le nombre actuel des juges est suffisant et qu'il serait dangereux de l'augmenter.

Ensuite, en ce qui concerne la durée du mandat des juges, il s'est demandé s'il fallait maintenir une nomination pour une durée relativement courte — six ans — ou s'il fallait envisager une nomination à vie.

Enfin, il a posé la question de l'opinion dissidente dont il s'est déclaré adversaire.

1. La représentation du Royaume-Uni

M. BEBR

Le professeur Jacobs semble souhaiter que la désignation des juges se fasse dans le cadre des *law districts*. Le Royaume-Uni serait le seul Etat membre qui pourrait profiter de ce mode de désignation. Cela me semble difficilement admissible.

---

* NDLR. Dans le présent compte rendu, les questions et les réponses ont été regroupées par thème. L'ordre chronologique des interventions n'a donc pas été respecté.

2. Le nombre des juges

M. EHLERMANN

La question du nombre des juges ne me semble pas du tout résolue. La Cour de justice elle-même a demandé récemment que le nombre des juges soit augmenté.

Sa proposition est en cours d'examen par les instances politiques.

M. GLAESNER

Avant de se prononcer sur le nombre des juges de la Cour et des chambres, il y a une option politique qui, à mon avis, doit être tranchée : la Cour de justice doit-elle demeurer un juge d'instance unique ou faut-il envisager d'instaurer un juge de première instance pour certaines affaires ?

M. MERTENS DE WILMARS

Je voudrais apporter quelques précisions purement factuelles.

Tout d'abord, en raison de l'adhésion de la Grèce, le nombre des juges de la Cour sera porté de neuf à dix.

Certains estiment probablement qu'on aurait dû saisir l'occasion pour une augmentation plus considérable.

Je n'examinerai pas cette question ici mais je voudrais revenir sur un point abordé par le professeur Jacobs (il va de soi que je parle en mon nom personnel). Il est exact que la balance entre des chambres de trois juges et une cour plénière de neuf juges n'est pas idéale. Lorsque la Cour comprendra dix juges, elle pourra constituer des chambres de cinq juges, ce qui rendrait possible de traiter au niveau des chambres des affaires que la Cour a réservées jusqu'ici aux audiences plénières.

Je crois que la Cour n'a pas cédé à la tentation de faire de la chambre à trois juges la composition normale de la Cour. Elle a veillé attentivement à ne pas confier aux chambres des affaires posant des problèmes nouveaux. Ce but n'est pas toujours atteint car des aspects nouveaux peuvent surgir au cours de l'instance, après le rapport préalable. Il appartient alors à la chambre de renvoyer l'affaire devant la cour plénière.

3. La durée de la nomination des juges

M. GOSSERIES

J'aurais voulu demander un renseignement d'ordre pratique : les juges de la Cour de justice ne sont-ils pas, en fait, pour la plupart, reconduits dans leurs fonctions de sorte que les nominations seraient, *de facto,* des nominations à vie ?

4. Les opinions dissidentes

M. BEBR

Je pense que le développement de la jurisprudence de la Cour n'a pas atteint un stade suffisant pour que l'on puisse accepter les opinions dissidentes. Après tout, moins de trente années, ce n'est pas une si longue période de temps ! Je crois que, pour le moment, la pratique des opinions dissidentes affaiblirait l'autorité des jugements de la Cour de justice.

Je préférerais des jugements moins *tranchés* mais qui nous donnent des orientations générales. Nous ne pouvons pas espérer, pour le moment, des jugements qui sont rédigés de la même façon que les jugements des juridictions nationales. Les solutions adoptées dans les ordres juridiques nationaux ne sont pas toujours transposables au niveau de la Communauté.

M. LAGRANGE

En 1950, au moment où le plan Schuman était examiné, la question des opinions dissidentes a été soulevée au comité juridique par le représentant des Pays-Bas qui était favorable à ces opinions dissidentes. Les autres délégations ont fait valoir que l'existence des avocats généraux permettrait à une personnalité indépendante d'exprimer une opinion qui pourrait être non conforme à celle de la Cour. La proposition du représentant des Pays-Bas n'a pas été retenue.

5. Réponse du rapporteur

Mr JACOBS

I am not sure that I can answer all the questions but I will comment on some points where there seems to have been disagreement. Purely by way of clarification on the question of the appointment of judges for a renewable term, I would say that it is clear that this concept of renewability is not compatible with the principle of judicial independence and that the members of the Court should be appointed for a non-renewable, longer term or perhaps for life. That seems to me an elementary proposition.

The question raised by Dr Glaesner about courts of first instance is much more difficult and I am not sure that it falls within my own province; it is really more a question of the "compétence de la Cour", but I would like to express my own view on this nonetheless. It does seem to me that the main task of the Court is to be a court of law rather than of fact and that therefore questions of fact should if possible be resolved in a tribunal of first instance with a possible appeal on questions of law to the Court of Justice. That has already been proposed in relation to staff cases and there have also been suggestions that it might be done in competiton cases and in other cases involving questions of fact.

I would actually like to go a little further. I would question whether, if such courts of first instance were established, there should be an automatic right of appeal to the Court on a point of law. Again my concern would be to limit the tasks of the Court to ensure that it is performing the fundamental constitutional tasks which it has in the Community and that it should not be submerged in a mass of cases of minor importance. And I would suggest that some lessons could be learnt here from the practice of the supreme courts in some of the Member States and certainly the Supreme Court of the United States in limiting access to the Court to cases of fundamental importance. So that if there were courts of first instance, I think that appeals on questions of law should be limited.

May I also say on this point that I think that the attitudes of many Community lawyers to these questions are influenced by considerations which are no longer relevant. There was a time when the Court did not have enough cases and when the main concern was that more cases should be referred to the Court. The position has changed and the Court can now afford to be a little more selective.

II. LA COMPOSITION DES CHAMBRES

M. GOFFIN, *président*

Nous pourrions examiner maintenant le deuxième groupe de questions qui a déjà été abordé indirectement.

Les principaux problèmes posés par le professeur Jacobs sont les suivants :

— y a-t-il un équilibre satisfaisant entre les affaires qui sont soumises à la Cour de justice siégeant en chambre de trois juges et les affaires traitées en séance plénière ?

— en particulier, une chambre de trois juges a-t-elle suffisamment d'autorité pour traiter certaines affaires ?

— faut-il nécessairement que siège un juge de l'Etat, comme c'est la règle, par exemple, pour la Cour européenne des droits de l'homme, ce qui implique une composition variable des chambres ?

M. GLAESNER

Différents problèmes doivent être distingués.

Dans certains domaines assez techniques, comme les droits de douane, les affaires sociales et même la concurrence, où il y a déjà une jurisprudence établie, les affaires pourraient être confiées à des chambres de trois juges. On pourrait prévoir un système de renvoi à la Cour plénière pour le cas où les chambres voudraient s'écarter de la jurisprudence établie.

Je ne crois pas indispensable qu'il y ait un juge de l'Etat intéressé.

D'ailleurs, il arrive que plusieurs Etats membres aient un intérêt particulier. C'est le cas dans les affaires de sécurité sociale de travailleurs migrants où sont impliqués les organismes de plusieurs Etats membres.

Parfois, au contraire, il n'y a pas d'Etat particulièrement intéressé, par exemple lorsque les deux parties au procès sont des institutions communautaires. Ces affaires relèvent d'ailleurs de la Cour plénière.

M. GOSSERIES

J'aimerais demander aux juges de la Cour de justice qui participent à ces travaux quelques précisions sur la façon dont les chambres sont constituées lorsque le litige soumis à la Cour porte sur des questions de sécurité sociale.

Etant donné la grande diversité des systèmes de sécurité sociale existant dans la Communauté, il semblerait normal que le juge ayant la nationalité de l'Etat membre dont le régime de sécurité sociale est en cause, soit désigné pour faire partie de la chambre. Par contre, cette désignation ne me paraît pas nécessaire — comme M. Glaesner vient de le dire — s'il y a déjà une jurisprudence sur la question.

Enfin, dans la mesure où l'affaire soulève des problèmes de principes généraux du droit, elle devrait être portée devant la Cour plénière.

III. LA REFORME DE LA PROCEDURE

M. PAULIN

Le professeur Jacobs a souligné à juste titre que les jugements de la Cour de justice devaient emporter l'adhésion des justiciables.

Il a émis une idée intéressante à propos des jugements rendus par la Cour de justice sur question préjudicielle des juridictions nationales. Il a suggéré que la Cour précise éventuellement les questions mal posées par les juridictions nationales et indique les points sur lesquels portera son jugement, de façon à permettre aux différentes parties d'intervenir utilement.

Il me semble que la Cour de justice a déjà, en pratique, retenu cette idée. Les cas dans lesquels la Cour interroge les parties sont de plus en plus fréquents. On a même vu, dans une affaire préjudicielle, la Cour poser des questions à un Etat membre qui, jusque-là n'était pas intervenu dans la procédure. Je fais allusion à l'affaire *Hansen* qui mettait en présence deux parties allemandes et dans laquelle le gouvernement allemand et la Commission étaient intervenus. La Cour, qui devait interpréter l'article 277, paragraphe 2 du traité, a jugé bon de questionner un Etat membre qui s'était désintéressé à tort de la procédure.

M. PESCATORE

Effectivement, au stade du « rapport préalable » présenté par le juge rapporteur — qui est un document interne —, la Cour s'interroge sur les problèmes juridiques posés par l'affaire et est amenée, de plus en plus souvent, à poser des questions aux parties.

M. Paulin a cité l'affaire *Hansen* où la Cour a essayé de connaître l'opinion du gouvernement français puisque le litige, qui jouait entre des parties allemandes, soulevait la question du statut des départements français d'outre-mer.

Je pense que la Cour serait bien inspirée de faire un usage plus fréquent de la clause de son statut, à savoir l'article 21, qui lui permet de demander l'opinion de tous les Etats membres et de toutes les institutions, même s'ils ne sont pas partie au procès.

La Cour utilise également d'autres moyens. Elle recourt plus fréquemment à des ruptures du délibéré, c'est-à-dire à une réouverture de la procédure pour éclaircir certaines questions qui étaient apparues lors d'une première phase des discussions.

Les arrêts interlocutoires, qui permettent au juge de fixer certains points de droit et de laisser ouvertes certaines questions qui sont encore insuffisamment élucidées, permettent également de circonscrire le débat. (*Rem.* : Voir à titre d'exemple l'arrêt du 27 février 1980, *Commission c. Royaume-Uni,* à propos du régime fiscal du vin).

Il me semble donc qu'il serait possible d'aller dans le sens souhaité par le professeur Jacobs en faisant un usage plus large des moyens offerts par le règlement de procédure de la Cour actuellement en vigueur, sans qu'il soit nécessaire de modifier celui-ci.

M. GOFFIN, *président*

Le délai de deux mois dans lequel les Etats membres peuvent intervenir ne devrait-il pas en tout cas être allongé ?

M. PESCATORE

Le délai de deux mois est fixé par le Statut de la Cour de justice qui fait partie intégrante du traité. Pour allonger ce délai, il faudrait donc modifier le traité, ce qui ne me paraît pas une perspective réaliste dans les conditions actuelles.

Mais les questions posées par la Cour sont précisément un moyen d'allonger ce délai. En effet, après l'expiration de celui-ci, vient la phase de l'instruction et la Cour peut très bien provoquer un deuxième échange de documents entre les parties en les interrogeant sur des aspects qui n'ont pas été suffisamment éclairés.

Au surplus, dans les procédures préjudicielles, les Etats membres ont la possibilité d'intervenir non seulement par écrit mais également oralement. Il est déjà arrivé que la Cour ait fait savoir à un gouvernement que ses intérêts étaient en jeu en attirant son attention sur le fait qu'il est loisible à une partie de comparaître à l'audience même si elle n'a pas participé à la procédure écrite.

Les règles de procédure actuelles permettent donc de résoudre dans une très large mesure les problèmes soulevés par le professeur Jacobs.

M. ALEXANDER

Je vais simplement citer un exemple pour illustrer ce que M. Pescatore vient de dire. La semaine dernière, la Cour de justice a réouvert une procédure préjudicielle en indiquant, non seulement aux parties au litige mais aussi aux Etats membres et aux institutions, certains points jurement juridiques sur lesquels la Cour aimerait que l'affaire soit replaidée.

M. MERTENS DE WILMARS

Avant l'audience, le juge rapporteur rédige un rapport d'audience qui est remis aux parties. Les plaideurs peuvent y trouver une série d'indications sur ce que peuvent être les préoccupations de la Cour.

Personnellement, je trouve qu'il serait souhaitable que les rapports d'audience indiquent de la façon la plus nette possible les questions qui paraissent importantes à la Cour, les parties ayant toujours la possibilité de faire valoir dans leurs plaidoiries qu'à leur avis le problème se pose dans d'autres termes.

Au début, la Cour avait adopté cette méthode. Le rapport d'audience ne se bornait pas à reproduire les arguments des parties, il les évaluait.

Il y a eu de nombreuses protestations de la part des parties qui estimaient que leurs arguments avaient été mal compris, si bien qu'aujourd'hui les rapports d'audience sont devenus la reproduction quasi-photographique des arguments échangés au cours de la procédure orale.

Il y a peut-être un équilibre à trouver entre ces deux méthodes, d'autant plus qu'en raison de la complexité croissante des affaires, les indications qui peuvent se trouver dans le rapport d'audience sont très précieuses pour les plaideurs.

M. GOFFIN, *président*

Le fait que le rapport d'audience soit distribué avant l'audience constitue un progrès par rapport à la procédure en vigueur devant le Conseil d'Etat belge puisque, dans celle-ci, le rapport d'audience n'est porté à la connaissance des parties qu'à l'audience même.

M. WAELBROECK

Je suis tout à fait d'accord qu'il serait utile que la Cour puisse indiquer à l'avance, dans le rapport d'audience, les points qui devraient faire l'objet de développements plus amples lors de la procédure orale, ce qui permettrait de donner à celle-ci un caractère plus dynamique.

Mais il ne faut pas oublier que le rapport d'audience, dans la mesure où il résume les arguments des plaideurs, fera partie de l'arrêt de la Cour de justice. Il me semble donc très important que l'argumentation des parties soit reproduite de la façon la plus fidèle possible.

Le rapport d'audience devrait donc comprendre deux parties qui doivent être soigneusement distinguées : le résumé de l'argumentation des parties et l'exposé des questions qui se posent.

Madame CUVELLIEZ

Je voudrais insister sur le fait qu'il est très intéressant pour l'individu-justiciable de trouver dans le rapport d'audience la liste des questions précises que la Cour souhaite éclaircir. L'individu ne dispose pas, comme les Etats membres ou comme les institutions de la Communauté, d'une infrastructure ou de moyens financiers lui permettant de se livrer à une exégèse approfondie du rapport d'audience pour essayer de deviner tous les problèmes juridiques qui pourraient surgir.

M. ALEXANDER

Je suis tout à fait d'accord avec le professeur Waelbroeck lorsqu'il dit que le rapport d'audience doit avant tout donner un résumé objectif des arguments invoqués. J'approuve également la proposition de compléter cet exposé par une énumération des questions qui devront être examinées.

Mais je voudrais ici attirer l'attention sur un problème technique qui, me semble-t-il, mérite d'être pris en considération.

Ma langue de travail est le hollandais. La plupart des documents fournis par la Cour de justice sont rédigés dans une autre langue et doivent donc être traduits, ce qui prend du temps. Je n'ai jamais reçu le rapport d'audience avant la veille de l'audience, en fin d'après-midi. Or les plaidoyers doivent se préparer longtemps à l'avance. Il faut faire des travaux de recherche, consulter les clients, etc. Le rapport d'audience devrait, à mon avis, être distribué trois ou quatre semaines avant l'audience.

M. GOFFIN, *président*

Un dernier problème pourrait peut-être retenir notre attention : celui de la modification du règlement de procédure. Le professeur Jacobs nous a rappelé que le règlement de procédure était établi par la Cour de justice et qu'il devait être approuvé à l'unanimité par le Conseil. Il s'est demandé s'il ne serait pas souhaitable que la Cour de justice consulte les praticiens avant de proposer une modification de son règlement de procédure. Je suggère, pour ma part, qu'elle demande l'avis de la Commission consultative des barreaux de la Communauté.

M. MERTENS DE WILMARS

La Cour de justice a pris contact avec les services juridiques des autres institutions de la Communauté et, ainsi que le souhaite M. Goffin, avec la Commission consultative des barreaux de la Communauté.

Réponse du rapporteur

M. JACOBS

This I feel is the most important part of my own subject: the elucidation of the questions which concern the Court before the oral hearing. I recognise of course that the Court has frequently put questions in advance of the oral hearing, questions to ascertain a particular point of fact which may be put to the Community institutions or to a Member State. But these are not at all the sort of questions which I have in mind.

What I am suggesting is that the Court should indicate the main issues which it sees to be relevant and that only in this way can the oral hearing serve a useful function and only in this way I would add, as I have said, can the judgments of the Court carry that final degree of conviction, at least for the parties and the Member States taking part.

I have in mind, for example, a case where an oral hearing lasted for two days and almost every conceivable issue on the case was argued but only at the end of the second day, rather late as sometimes happens, at seven o'clock in the evening, did a question emerge from the Court which in time proved to be the decisive issue on which the case was eventually decided.

I would also emphasise that the suggestion I make does not involve any amendement of the rules of procedure, it does not involve any amendment of the Statute of the Court; on the contrary, it seems to me that if a greater use of the oral hearing were made in this way, it would not be necessary to extend the period for submitting written observations. This would be an alternative method of meeting the concern of practitioners and of the Member States.

Again, of course, another possibility would be for the judges, if this were appropriate, to give an indication at an earlier stage in the oral hearing itself or possibly to adjourn the oral hearing for a short period so that the issues which had emerged as being of particular interest could then be argued a little more fully after a short adjournment.

So it does seem to me that within the present framework of the procedure, there are ample means of satisfying the requirements of justice as a United Kingdom practitioner would see them and that this would be particularly feasible if the overall work of the Court were not increased by an undue increase in its case-load. It would then be possible for the Court to be — as we all expect it to be — a final court dealing with cases of fundamental importance to the Community, giving most careful consideration to those relatively few cases with which it would have to deal and to decide those cases with proper weight for the Community interest and the interest of the parties.

LES ETATS MEMBRES ET LA COMPETENCE DE LA COUR

par

Robert KOVAR,

Professeur à la Faculté de droit et des sciences politiques de l'Université de Strasbourg,
Directeur des Etudes juridiques au Collège d'Europe.

Aux termes de l'article 4 du traité de la CEE, la Cour de justice est l'une des *institutions* chargées de « la réalisation des tâches confiées à la Communauté » (1). Organe judiciaire, elle n'en est pas moins ainsi amenée nécessairement à se définir par rapport au projet d'ensemble de l'intégration qu'il appartient à chacune des institutions communautaires de promouvoir selon sa nature propre (2). La perception de cette exigence essentielle lui confère une condition spécifique dépassant de loin celle d'une juridiction internationale.

Les fonctions assumées par la Cour entretiennent des relations nécessairement intimes avec les caractères fondamentaux de l'ordre juridique communautaire. La Communauté est un groupement d'Etats dont le principe réside dans « l'obéissance de tous aux mêmes lois » (3). En l'absence de tout appareil de coercition, l'autorité du droit communautaire ne saurait procéder que de la conviction de la nécessité de respecter la règle commune indissociable d'une exacte appréciation des intérêts de chacun des Etats et de la Communauté. Sans elle, « l'ordre juridique de la Communauté perdrait son caractère communautaire », « la base juridique de la Communauté » en serait affectée et, finalement, « la notion de Communauté » serait elle-même compromise (4). Mais la Communauté est davantage qu'une organisation interétatique. Elle « constitue un nouvel ordre juridique (...) dont les sujets sont non seulement les Etats membres mais également leurs ressortissants » (5). L'intégration postule donc aussi bien la subordination des droits nationaux au droit communautaire que la pénétration de celui-ci dans l'ordonnancement juridique étatique de manière qu'il puisse y déployer la

(1) Traité CEEA, article 3.

(2) Voy. dans ce sens W.J. Ganshof van der Meersch, L'ordre juridique des Communautés européennes et le droit international, *RCADI*, 1975, V, p. 267.

(3) R. Lecourt, *L'Europe des juges*, E. Bruylant, Bruxelles, 1976, p. 221.

(4) Voy. arrêt *Costa c. ENEL*, 18 juillet 1964, affaire 6-64, *Rec.*, 1964, p. 1160 et suiv.

(5) Voy. arrêt *Van Gend en Loos*, 5 février 1963, affaire 26-62, *Rec.*, 1962, p. 1 et suiv.

plénitude de ses effets. Enfin, les traités communautaires sont créateurs d'institutions dotées d'amples pouvoirs dont l'exercice affecte tant les Etats que leurs ressortissants.

Cette complexion « pluridimensionnelle » (6) de la Communauté exige que la Cour de justice soit à même de contrôler l'action de ses institutions, de veiller au respect des engagements des Etats, enfin d'assurer l'effectivité du droit communautaire. L'ampleur et la nature des compétences de la Cour exprime l'intégration juridique réalisée dans la Communauté comme elle en révèle les limites.

Chargée d'assurer le respect du droit dans l'interprétation et l'application des traités, la Cour est investie « d'une mission vaste et fondamentale qui, d'emblée, se situe au-delà du seul règlement des litiges entre les différents protagonistes de l'ordre juridique communautaire » (7). Ainsi l'existence d'un véritable pouvoir judiciaire est assurément la différence la plus marquante qui sépare les Communautés européennes des organisations internationales. La Cour de justice est une juridiction unique, permanente, obligatoire et souveraine. De plus, elle peut être saisie non seulement par les Etats ou les institutions mais encore par les ressortissants de la Communauté. Pour autant, la Cour n'a que des compétences d'attribution. Elle est, en un certain sens du terme, une juridiction d'exception, le juge communautaire de droit commun étant, par l'action conjuguée de ce principe et de celui de l'effet direct, le juge national.

Restituer la fonction judiciaire dans la Communauté exige donc qu'elle soit envisagée dans ces deux dimensions. D'où la nécessité de commencer par l'examen de l'aménagement de la compétence juridictionnelle dans la Communauté, pour pouvoir ensuite étudier l'agencement des compétences de la Cour de justice considérées en elles-mêmes.

I. L'AMENAGEMENT DES COMPETENCES JURIDICTIONNELLES DANS LA COMMUNAUTE

La répartition des compétences juridictionnelles dans les Communautés s'organise autour de trois considérations essentielles. Tout d'abord, la nécessité d'assurer l'autonomie des institutions communautaires qui, dans certains cas, suppose l'attribution à la Cour de compétences exclusives. Ensuite, la nécessité pratique mais aussi politique, de recourir à une justice décentralisée

---

(6) L.J. Constantinesco, *Dix ans de jurisprudence de la Cour de justice des Communautés européennes*, Cologne, Colloque 1965, Heymanns Verlag, p. 204.

(7) G. Vandersanden et A. Barav, *Contentieux communautaire*, E. Bruylant, Bruxelles, 1977, p. 3.

conservant aux juridictions nationales leurs fonctions naturelles. Cette dernière considération est tempérée par l'exigence de l'unité et de l'uniformité du droit communautaire d'où procède la compétence interprétative de la Cour de justice. Il en résulte une combinaison complexe de compétences les unes exclusives, les autres concurrentes, les dernières enfin partagées, destinées à assurer l'autonomie de la Communauté et à préserver celle des Etats dans le respect dû au droit communautaire.

A) L'agencement des compétences juridictionnelles et l'autonomie des institutions de la Communauté

L'autonomie de la Communauté exige que les juridictions nationales ne puissent contrôler la légalité des décisions prises par ses institutions ou engager leur responsabilité. Cette exigence a conduit à reconnaître à la Cour une série de compétences exclusives. C'est ainsi que le contentieux de la légalité (recours en annulation, recours en carence, exception d'illégalité) comme celui de la responsabilité extracontractuelle lui appartiennent en propre. La faculté de réserver la compétence de la Cour pour connaître du contentieux de la responsabilité contractuelle (8) de même que l'aménagement de la responsabilité des agents de la Communauté procède de la même préoccupation (9).

Plus contestable est assurément la possibilité reconnue par l'article 177 du traité de la CEE (10) aux juridictions nationales, du moins à celles ne statuant pas en dernier ressort, de se prononcer sur la validité des actes des institutions de la Communauté. Comme l'écrit G. Bebr, « la liberté laissée aux juridictions inférieures (de demander ou non à la Cour de Justice l'examen de la validité de l'acte) est regrettable et ne se justifie pas dans le cadre de l'examen en validité » (11). Un tel pouvoir va à l'encontre de la compétence exclusive de la Cour en matière de contrôle de la légalité, du principe de l'uniformité d'application et de validité des actes dans l'ordre juridique de la Communauté, de la primauté du droit communautaire enfin. Le professeur Ganshof van der Meersch (12) invoque encore d'autres raisons. Il souligne, notamment, « le danger de voir le juge national sacrifier à la thèse de l'" acte clair " ». Il relève aussi combien il est anormal qu'un juge

---

(8) La Cour n'est appelée à en connaître qu'en vertu d'une clause compromissoire: traité CEE, article 181; traité CEEA, article 153; traité CECA, article 42.

(9) Voy. affaire 9-69, *Sayag et autres c. Leduc et autres*, arrêt du 10/7/1969, *Rec.*, 1969, p. 239 et suiv.

(10) Article 150 du traité de la CEEA.

(11) G. Bebr, Examen en validité au titre de l'article 177 du traité CEE et cohésion juridique de la Communauté, *Cah. dr. eur.*, 1975, p. 379 et suiv., spéc. p. 381.

(12) *Op. cit.*, p. 321.

national soit en droit de refuser l'application d'un acte de l'une des institutions sans que celle-ci soit partie à la cause et puisse en justifier le fondement juridique. D'où la conclusion qu'il est « difficile de concilier avec l'esprit des traités malgré l'apparent parallélisme des procédures qui gouvernent l'interprétation et l'examen de la validité des actes des institutions, le fait de soustraire pareille décision à l'inappréciable garantie que constitue pour la cohérence du droit communautaire la décision de la Cour de Justice » ([13]). De nombreux autres auteurs regrettent également la confusion de deux renvois aussi différents par leur objet dans une seule procédure ([14]). G. Bebr va plus loin pour sa part puisqu'il s'efforce de limiter au plus près les prérogatives des juridictions nationales. La discrétion laissée à celle qui ne statue pas en dernier ressort doit être réduite « soit à reconnaître la validité d'un acte et, en conséquence, à l'appliquer, soit, si elle a des doutes sur sa validité, à surseoir à statuer et à saisir la Cour » ([15]). D'autres auteurs se prononcent de *lege ferenda* en faveur de la compétence exclusive de la Cour de justice pour apprécier la validité d'un acte d'une institution de la Communauté ([16]). Il suffirait de s'inspirer de l'article 41 du traité de la CECA qui se lit comme suit :

> *« La Cour est seule compétente pour statuer, à titre préjudiciel sur la validité des délibérations de la Haute Autorité et du Conseil, dans le cas où un litige porté devant un tribunal national mettrait en cause cette validité. »*

Telle est précisément la suggestion formulée par la Cour de justice dans sa contribution au rapport sur l'Union européenne où elle estime qu'« une disposition devrait prévoir qu'une juridiction nationale ne puisse considérer un acte communautaire comme privé de validité que si la Cour, préalablement saisie, a statué en ce sens » ([17]).

Pour le reste, les compétences juridictionnelles de la Cour de justice ont trait essentiellement à l'interprétation du droit communautaire et au contrôle du respect des obligations des Etats. La compétence interprétative est partagée entre elle et les juridictions nationales. Celles-ci, du moins

---

(13) *Ibid.*

(14) Voy. notamment J. Boulouis et R.M. Chevallier, *Grands arrêts de la Cour de justice des Communautés européennes*, Dalloz, 1er éd., Tome 1, p. 111.

(15) Article précité p. 384.

(16) Voy. A. Donner, « Les rapports entre la compétence de la Cour de Justice des Communautés européennes et les tribunaux nationaux », RCADI, 1975, II, p. 3 et suiv., spéc. p. 39; Ch. Tomuschat, *Die gerichtliche Vorabentscheidung nach den Verträgen über die europäischen Gemeinschaften*, Berlin, 1964, p. 202 et suiv. A. Pepy, Le rôle des juridictions nationales dans l'application de l'article 177 et la jurisprudence de la Cour de Justice, *Cah. dr. eur.*, 1966, p. 21 et suiv., spéc. p. 34.

(17) *Bull. CE*, suppl. 9/75, p. 21.

lorsqu'elles ne statuent pas en dernier ressort, ont compétence pour interpréter le droit communautaire, même si elles peuvent, en vertu de l'article 177 du traité de la CEE ([18]), préférer saisir la Cour d'une question préjudicielle. Les juridictions souveraines sont, en revanche, tenues de renvoyer toute question d'interprétation nouvelle à la seule exception de celle dépourvue manifestement de sérieux ou de pertinence. L'économie comme la raison d'être de cette procédure est indissociable d'une conception décentralisée de l'exercice de la fonction judiciaire dans la Communauté, respectueuse de l'autonomie des Etats dans la mesure où elle ne compromet pas l'efficacité du droit communautaire.

B) L'agencement des compétences juridictionnelles et l'autonomie des Etats de la Communauté

La décentralisation de la fonction juridictionnelle dans la Communauté met en évidence un décalage caractéristique entre l'immédiateté normative dont on sait qu'elle a atteint un degré de perfectionnement remarquable et, en parallèle, une incontestable carence de l'immédiateté judiciaire. Cette carence se traduit d'abord par l'absence d'insertion directe des juridictions nationales dans une hiérarchie judiciaire communautaire. La seule articulation existante est celle de l'article 177. Cette carence se traduit encore par l'absence d'un accès direct des justiciables devant la Cour de justice par le biais d'un recours contre les décisions des tribunaux des Etats membres de la Communauté. C'est dire, dans un tel contexte, l'importance de la procédure du renvoi préjudiciel en interprétation et de la qualité des relations entre les juridictions nationales et la Cour de justice. Mais, précisément, l'économie de cette procédure est signifiante, tout à la fois, de la répartition des compétences juridictionnelles dans la Communauté et de l'absence de subordination organique des juridictions nationales à l'autorité judiciaire de la Communauté.

La Cour de justice s'est constamment préoccupée de pallier cette absence d'immédiatisation judiciaire par le développement de l'effet direct du droit communutaire, par le refus d'admettre toute limititation abusive à la faculté donnée aux juridictions nationales d'user du renvoi en interprétation ([19]), par une définition toujours plus exigeante des effets des normes directement applicables entraînant une « communautarisation » de l'office des juges nationaux dès lors que l'autonomie institutionnelle ne permet pas

---

([18]) Traité CEEA, article 150.

([19]) Voy. arrêts du 27 octobre 1971, *Rheinmühlen*, affaires 6-79, *Rec.* 1971, p. 823 et suiv. et 166-73, 16 janvier 1974, *Rec.*, 1974, p. 335.

d'assurer l'efficacité pleine et entière du droit communautaire ([20]). Par ce biais, la Cour a cherché à reconstituer une certaine immédiateté procédurale alignée sur la cohérence de l'immédiateté normative. On est cependant en droit de se demander si cette démarche ne tend pas à épuiser ses possibilités ([21]) et si une autre approche ne devrait pas être envisagée. Elle consisterait à introduire une certaine immédiatisation directe des relations judiciaires dans la Communauté. Tel nous paraît être le sens des diverses propositions qui ont été faites par la doctrine mais aussi par des autorités qualifiées dont nous rendrons compte dans la suite de ces développements.

Conformément au principe de décentralisation judiciaire, seules les juridictions nationales ont à connaître des litiges opposant les particuliers entre eux ou aux instances étatiques alors même que ce contentieux aurait incidemment voire même principalement pour objet l'application du droit communautaire ([22]). Son effectivité dépend donc largement d'elles. Aussi s'avère-t-il particulièrement nécessaire de réserver à la Cour de justice la compétence de veiller à l'unité d'interprétation du droit communautaire, encore que celle-ci n'est amenée à intervenir que dans les limites du renvoi préjudiciel de l'article 177. Ces limites tiennent d'abord à la dissociation de l'application et de l'interprétation du droit communautaire ([23]). Elles tiennent surtout à ce que cette procédure ne procède pas d'un principe de subordination hiérarchique mais d'un esprit de collaboration dans le respect mutuel des compétences des juridictions nationales et de la Cour des Communautés ([24]). La question d'interprétation ne fait pas l'objet d'un recours. C'est une question soulevée dans le cadre d'une procédure non contentieuse que seules les juridictions peuvent poser à la Cour. Si sa décision s'impose au juge interne en vertu de l'« autorité de la chose interprétée », aucune sanction, sinon celle, indirecte, de l'article 169, ne saurait contraindre les juridictions suprêmes au respect de l'obligation de saisir la Cour et à celle de se conformer à ses arrêts. Enfin, la condition des justi-

---

([20]) V. notamment affaire 48-71 *Commission c. République italienne*, 13 juillet 1971, *Rec.*, 1972, p. 529 et suiv. et affaire 106-77, *Simmenthal*, 9 mars 1978, *Rec.*, 1978, p. 629 et suiv.

([21]) Voy. à cet égard aff. no 53-76, *Rewe*, 16 décembre 1976, *Rec.*, 1976, p. 1989 et suiv. et nº 45-76, *Comet*, 16 décembre 1976, *Rec.*, 1976, p. 2043 et suiv.

([22]) Pour une exception, voy. article 16 du Protocole sur les privilèges et immunités de la Communauté; arrêt *Humblet c. Belgique*, affaire 6-60, 16 décembre 1960, *Rec.*, 1960, p. 1127 et suiv.

([23]) Voy. Rapport MERCHIERS sur les problèmes posés par l'article 177 du traité CEE, Commission juridique du Parlement européen, 15 septembre 1969, document nº 94, nº 6.

([24]) Dans son arrêt 13-68, *Salgoil* du 19 décembre 1968, *Rec.*, 1968, p. 611 et suiv., la Cour a souligné que la procédure de l'article 177 repose sur le principe d'une nette séparation des fonctions.

ciables demeure essentiellement médiatisée. Ainsi se révèlent les implications du partage des compétences judiciaires, expression du degré d'intégration juridique réalisé dans la Communauté.

Pour sa part, la Cour s'est efforcée de ne pas outrepasser les limites de sa compétence tout en assurant au renvoi préjudiciel en interprétation son efficacité maximale. C'est ainsi qu'elle s'interdit d'appliquer la règle communautaire à l'espèce en vidant le litige au principal (25), et, *a fortiori*, de se prononcer sur le sens ou la validité d'une disposition nationale. La démarcation entre l'interprétation et l'application est pourtant souvent ténue. Aussi, soucieuse de ne pas la transgresser, la Cour a constamment recommandé aux juridictions nationales de formuler leurs questions en des termes suffisamment « abstraits ». Si légitime qu'elle soit, cette préoccupation ne signifie néanmoins pas que la Cour en vienne à livrer une interprétation privée de toute valeur opérative en raison d'une abstraction exagérée. Aussi ne saurait-elle ignorer entièrement les faits de l'espèce. En revanche, elle excéderait sa compétence en vérifiant l'adéquation de ces données à la règle interprétée. On conçoit mieux comment s'organise, autour de l'élément factuel, la distinction nécessairement subtile, de l'interprétation et de l'application qui gouverne l'économie de la procédure du renvoi et par là même le rôle respectif des juges nationaux et communautaires. Equilibre délicat qui ne peut être préservé que par leur coopération confiante.

La Cour de justice doit aussi se garder d'interpréter et de qualifier les règles nationales. Dans ce cas encore, elle se prémunit contre une attitude qui consisterait à prétendre pouvoir ignorer complètement la norme nationale qui, précisément, se trouve généralement au centre du litige soumis au juge national. La Cour se soucie à nouveau d'apporter au juge l'assistance la plus efficace sans, pour autant, se substituer à lui. Aussi accueille-t-elle toutes les précisions qui lui sont fournies à cet égard par la juridiction qui est à l'origine du renvoi. Au total, une interprétation souple de la séparation des fonctions des juges communautaire et national est la condition de l'efficacité de la « coopération judiciaire par laquelle juridiction nationale et Cour de Justice, dans l'ordre de leurs compétences propres, sont appelées à contribuer directement et réciproquement à l'élaboration d'une décision en vue d'assurer l'application uniforme du droit communautaire dans l'ensemble des Etats membres » (26).

La qualité indéniable des résultats obtenus n'exclut pas la possibilité d'apporter des améliorations à la procédure du renvoi préjudiciel en inter-

(25) Voy., par exemple, 15 juillet 1964, affaire 100-63, *Van der Veen*, *Rec.*, 1964, p. 1065 et suiv., conclusions M. Lagrange.

(26) 1er décembre 1965, affaire 16-65, *Firma Schwarze*, *Rec.*, 1965, p. 1081 et suiv., conclusions J. Gand.

prétation. Le refus de certaines juridictions suprêmes de s'adresser à la Cour en recourant abusivement à des procédés tels que celui de l'« acte clair », la méconnaissance, parfois délibérée, de l'autorité de la chose interprétée sont autant de raisons pour envisager le renforcement de cette procédure qui, par-delà sa fonction première, contribue à assurer une protection indirecte aux droits des ressortissants communautaires (27). Certes, l'utilisation de l'article 169 du traité de la CEE ne doit pas être écartée même si sa mise en œuvre s'avérait délicate (28) mais les justiciables n'y trouveraient de toute façon qu'imparfaitement leur compte d'abord parce qu'ils n'ont pas la maîtrise de cette procédure, ensuite parce que l'exécution de la décision de la Cour serait malaisée. Aussi les remèdes proposés consistent à prévoir soit une procédure obligatoire de constatation de manquement, par un recours des parties contre toute décision d'une juridiction nationale qui aurait manqué à saisir la Cour alors qu'elle y serait obligée (29), soit à accorder aux parties intéressées un droit d'appel à la Cour contre les arrêts des juridictions nationales ayant tranché sans avoir saisi la Cour alors même qu'elles ne seraient pas tenues de le faire (30). Comme le souligne la Commission : « la première solution est la plus rigoureuse parce qu'elle sanctionne toute violation de la procédure « 177 » mais est limitée au cas où le renvoi par la juridiction nationale est obligatoire, la seconde a, par contre, l'avantage de donner le dernier mot à la Cour de justice dans tous les cas sans qu'elle doive relever un manquement du juge national ».

Toutes ces suggestions ont en commun d'entraîner une inflexion de la nature de la procédure du renvoi en interprétation. Elle résulterait tant de l'introduction d'une certaine subordination hiérarchique dans des relations de collaboration que de l'intervention des parties se substituant à une coopération judiciaire défaillante. Il n'est pas certain que ces solutions soient opportunes et encore moins qu'elles puissent recevoir un accueil favorable.

D'autres procèdent de la même inspiration mais lui donnent cependant une expression plus atténuée. Tel est le cas des suggestions émanant d'origines diverses d'introduire une sorte de recours « dans l'intérêt de la

(27) Voy., R. Kovar, Le droit des personnes privées à obtenir devant la Cour des Communautés le respect du droit communautaire par les Etats membres, *AFDI*, 1966, p. 509 et suiv.

(28) Voy., entre autres, la réponse de la Commission à la question écrite nº 349/69 de M. Westerterp, 10 novembre 1969, *JOCE*, nº C 20 du 14 février 1970, p. 3.

(29) Rapport sur l'Union européenne, précité.

(30) Rapport sur l'Union européenne, *Bull. CE*, supplément 5/75, p. 37

loi » ([31]) inspiré du pourvoi dans l'intérêt de la loi qui existe dans plusieurs droits nationaux. Sa mise en œuvre pourrait être confiée aux avocats généraux la Cour de justice ([32]). Cette procédure se différencierait de celles prévues par certaines conventions attribuant compétence interprétative à la Cour des Communautés. Le pourvoi est, en effet, alors exercé par le procureur général près la juridiction suprême ou toute autre autorité désignée par les Etats contractants ([33]). L'intérêt d'un tel pourvoi serait de lier les juridictions nationales pour l'avenir en renforçant l'autorité des arrêts déjà rendus sur des questions préjudicielles même s'il n'en résultait aucune remise en cause des décisions à l'occasion desquelles l'interprétation serait demandée ([34]).

Non sans hésitation, les Etats membres ont admis l'utilité d'étendre la compétence interprétative de la Cour de justice à diverses conventions en rapport avec les objectifs de la Communauté. A cette fin, des protocoles ont organisé des procédures de questions préjudicielles inspirées de l'article 177 du traité de la CEE mais s'en différenciant à certains égards ([35]). Tout en se louant de ces attributions de compétences, on se doit de regretter les restrictions dont elles sont assorties. On ne saurait donc suivre ceux qui ont pu se féliciter de ce que la formulation donnée à l'article 3 du protocole du 3 juin 1971 laissait aux juridictions suprêmes la possibilité de refuser quasi-discrétionnairement la saisine de la Cour de justice ([36]). Au contraire, il serait souhaitable d'unifier ces procédures en les alignant sur la formule la plus favorable à la compétence de la Cour, donc à l'unité du droit dans la Communauté. Davantage, il conviendrait d'étendre sa compétence interprétative à toutes les conventions « commerciales » susceptibles d'avoir des répercussions même indirectes sur le fonctionnement de la Communauté ([37]).

([31]) Voy. Rapport MERCHIERS, précité et aussi PETERHAY, Une approche politique de l'application de l'article 177 du Traité CEE par les juridictions nationales, *Cah. dr. eur.*, 1971, p. 503 et suiv., M. WAELBROECK, FIDE, Sixième congrès international, Luxembourg, 24-26 Mai 1973, *Jurisprudence sur les problèmes généraux de l'intégration*, Rapport belge, ronéo, p. 35.

([32]) Voy. P. GORI, L'avocat général à la Cour de Justice, *Cah. dr. eur.*, 1976, p. 378 et suiv., spéc. p. 389, nº 111.

([33]) Voy. article 4, paragraphe 1 du protocole concernant l'interprétation par la Cour de justice de la convention du 27 septembre 1968 concernant la compétence judiciaire et l'exécution des décisions en matière civile et commerciale.

([34]) Pour une discussion de la portée de l'arrêt de la Cour de justice, voy. A.L. DROZ, La Cour de Justice des Communautés européennes et les conflits de juridictions à l'intérieur du Marché Commun, *AFDI*, 1977, p. 902 et suiv., spéc. p. 908.

([35]) Voy. protocole du 3 juin 1971, précité, articles 1, 2 et 3; protocole du 3 juin 1971 concernant l'interprétation par la Cour de Justice de la convention du 29 février 1968 sur la reconnaissance mutuelle des sociétés et des personnes morales, articles 1 et 2; convention relative au brevet européen pour le marché commun, article 73.

([36]) Voy. A.L. DROZ, article précité, p. 903.

([37]) Voy. en ce sens rapport de la Cour de Justice, précité, p. 19 et suiv. En effet, les échanges intra-communautaires pourraient souffrir d'interprétations divergentes de conventions commerciales sur les effets de commerce ou sur la vente commerciale.

Il a été parfois souhaité d'aller plus avant encore en envisageant d'ouvrir aux ressortissants communautaires certaines possibilités d'agir directement devant la Cour à l'encontre de décisions des instances nationales prises en violation du droit communautaire. Cette suggestion a été émise spécialement à propos des droits fondamentaux protégés dans la Communauté dans le cadre d'une éventuelle union européenne. Leur concrétisation est évidemment subordonnée à la réalisation de progrès dans cette voie.

II. L'AGENCEMENT DES COMPETENCES JURIDICTIONNELLES DE LA COUR DE JUSTICE DE LA COMMUNAUTE

Envisagées en elles-mêmes, les compétences de la Cour de justice doivent permettre de satisfaire à plusieurs exigences. La première est de lui procurer les moyens de remplir sa mission constitutionnelle, c'est-à-dire de veiller au respect des traités par les institutions de la Communauté. Il lui revient aussi de protéger les ressortissants communautaires contre les empiétements illégaux que celles-ci peuvent commettre. Il lui incombe, enfin, de rappeler les Etats à l'observance de la loi commune. D'où un ensemble complexe de procédures qui s'inscrivent dans le cadre du contentieux de la légalité, du contentieux de l'indemnité ou encore du contentieux de la constatation des manquements. Leur agencement n'est pas parfaitement homogène. La comparaison des traités de Paris et de Rome révèle des différences appréciables. Une unification serait assurément la bienvenue, à condition qu'elle se fasse par alignement sur un « standard maximum de protection ». Leur examen laisse apparaître, en outre, d'incontestables déficiences susceptibles de s'aggraver, en particulier, sous l'effet des modifications acquises, en cours ou concevables affectant le système institutionnel de la Communauté. Ces dysfonctions appellent des corrections.

A) Les compétences juridictionnelles de la Cour de justice et le contrôle de constitutionnalité dans la Communauté

L'étendue du contrôle de constitutionnalité de la Cour peut être regardée comme insuffisante à certains égards. Ce contrôle s'exerce par le biais du recours en annulation à l'encontre des seules décisions du Conseil et de la Commission [38]. L'institutionnalisation du Conseil européen pourrait conduire à envisager son assujettissement à ce contrôle. Les principes énoncés par la Cour dans son arrêt *AETR* paraissent certainement transposables.

---

[38] Traité CEE, article 173; traité CEEA, article 146; traité CECA, article 33 qui n'ouvre le recours en annulation que contre les décisions et recommandations de la Haute Autorité.

Organiquement, rien n'interdit de voir dans le Conseil européen une formation particulière du Conseil des ministres. Aussi, dès lors que ses délibérations portent « sur un objet qui relève de la compétence de la Communauté », elle ne peut se situer « hors du cadre des institutions communes ». Si ces délibérations « visent à produire des effets de droit », elles doivent pouvoir faire l'objet d'un recours en annulation [39]. Pareille conclusion doit évidemment être relativisée par des considérations tenant à la conception qu'a le Conseil européen de son rôle. Néanmoins, même sous ce rapport, on se doit de rappeler que le communiqué publié à l'issue de la réunion des chefs d'Etat ou de gouvernement, tenue à Paris les 9 et 10 décembre 1974, annonçant la création du « Conseil européen » témoigne de sa nature double : « Les chefs de gouvernement ont, (...), décidé de se réunir, accompagnés des ministres des affaires étrangères, trois fois par an et chaque fois que nécessaire, en Conseil de la Communauté et au titre de la coopération politique ».

On notera dans le même sens une déclaration du Conseil des ministres de la Communauté du 7 octobre 1976 :

> « *Les décisions que le Conseil européen a prises jusqu'à présent dans le domaine relevant des traités communautaires étaient de nature politique et n'avaient pas pour objet de créer par elles-mêmes des effets juridiques. Le cas échéant, le Conseil européen, en respectant les dispositions des traités, peut néanmoins prendre en tant que Conseil des Communautés des décisions portant effet juridique* » [40].

Il apparaît ensuite que, sous réserve de l'article 38 du traité de la CECA, les délibérations du Parlement lui échappent. Certains ont pu s'en émouvoir, craignant l'absence de garanties contre d'éventuels débordements de l'Assemblée. Le juge Pescatore s'est efforcé de démontrer que ces appréhensions étaient sans fondement, la Cour de justice étant en mesure d'assurer le contrôle des délibérations du Parlement [41]. Selon lui, la lacune de l'article 173 ne serait qu'apparence puisqu'elle procéderait de l'idée « de la non possibilité d'actes juridiques du Parlement » [42]. En vérité, cette disposition exprimerait « l'intention d'établir un contrôle de la légalité générale sur les actes émanant des institutions qui, dans le système du traité, apparaissent comme étant les seuls détenteurs du pouvoir de règlement, de

---

(39) Affaire 22-70, *Commission c. Conseil*, 31 mars 1971, *Rec.*, 1971, p. 263 et suiv.

(40) Réponse à la question écrite n° 293/76 de M. Guerlin, *JOCE* du 15 novembre 1976, n° C 269, p. 6. Voy. également la réponse à la question écrite n° 294/76 du même, *JOCE* du 13 décembre 1976, n° C 294 p. 4 et suiv.

(41) P. Pescatore, Reconnaissance et contrôle judiciaire des actes du Parlement européen, *Rev. trim. dr. eur.*, 1978, p. 581 et suiv.

(42) Voy. P. Pescatore, article précité, p. 586.

directive et de décision » ([43]). Aussi conviendrait-il de considérer que « l'article 173 vise à instituer un contrôle de légalité complet, une protection juridique sans discontinuité en faveur de tous ceux qui sont investis d'un droit d'action, à savoir les Etats membres, le Conseil et la Commission ([44]). Conception qui serait conforme au prescrit de l'article 164 qui confie à la Cour de justice pour mission d'assurer « le respect du droit dans l'interprétation et l'application du (...) traité ». L'éminent auteur parvient ainsi à une alternative : « ou bien le pouvoir constituant de la Communauté, c'est-à-dire la collectivité des Etats membres, qui détient l'exercice du droit de révision, consent à introduire dans le traité des dispositions destinées à permettre un contrôle juridictionnel sur les actes du Parlement ; ou bien, à défaut d'une telle initiative, on ne pourra éviter qu'un jour la Cour de justice à la suite d'une plainte introduite par un Etat membre, par le Conseil ou par la Commission, soit affrontée au difficile et fondamental problème que nous venons d'esquisser » ([45]). En pareil cas, le Parlement pourrait soulever une exception d'irrecevabilité en invoquant éventuellement les termes de l'article 173 ou, argument plus douteux, sa « souveraineté ». Il pourrait aussi accepter la compétence de la Cour de justice. Celle-ci serait dès lors à même d'accueillir le recours. Ces considérations sont certes essentiellement spéculatives, encore que l'accroissement des pouvoirs budgétaires du Parlement leur donne une certaine consistance. On relèvera que, dans sa contribution à ce qu'il convient d'appeler le rapport Tindemans, la Cour a estimé que : « Dans l'hypothèse où l'Union européenne comporterait un Parlement élu exerçant un pouvoir législatif, surgirait la question d'un éventuel contrôle de conformité au traité des actes législatifs. La Cour de justice aurait alors vocation à exercer un tel contrôle » ([46]).

Le contrôle des actes du Parlement pourrait aussi être exercé par le biais du renvoi préjudiciel en appréciation de validité qui confère à la Cour compétence pour se prononcer sur la validité « des actes pris par les institutions de la Communauté ». Cette procédure ne satisfait cependant pas entièrement aux conditions d'un contrôle de constitutionnalité en raison des modalités de sa mise en œuvre.

A l'inverse, l'Assemblée est privée de possibilités d'agir devant la Cour à l'encontre des autres institutions. L'article 173, outre les personnes privées, n'ouvre le recours en annulation qu'aux Etats, au Conseil et à la Commission. L'article 175 est pour le moins ambigu ([47]). Pourtant, ici

---

([43]) P. Pescatore, article précité, p. 587.

([44]) P. Pescatore, *ibid.*

([45]) P. Pescatore, *ibid.*

([46]) Voy. rapport précité, p. 17 et suiv.

([47]) Voy. G. Vandersanden et A. Barav, *Contentieux communautaire*, Bruylant, Bruxelles, 1977, p. 238.

encore, il est évident que le Parlement peut s'affronter au Conseil ou à la Commission dans de graves différends constitutionnels. Les incidents qui, en 1978 et en 1979, ont marqué la procédure budgétaire en portent témoignage. Aussi ne s'étonne-t-on pas de constater que le Parlement ait revendiqué l'accès à ces deux procédures ([48]).

B) Les compétences juridictionnelles de la Cour de justice et la protection des administrés dans la Communauté

Cette protection est assurée par des voies de droit diversifiées qui permettent aux ressortissants communautaires de contester la légalité des décisions des institutions de la Communauté ou d'engager leur responsabilité. La protection ainsi assurée est certainement appréciable même si elle comporte des restrictions parfois excessives. Il en est ainsi des limites établies par l'article 173, alinéa 2 à l'exercice par les « requérants non privilégiés » du recours en annulation. Elles ont été souvent regrettées en certaines circonstances par la Cour de justice elle-même. Ce n'est certainement pas le lieu pour analyser sa jurisprudence relative à l'article 173, alinéa 2. On se contentera de souligner que le développement des mesures d'intervention spécialement dans le cadre de la politique agricole commune a multiplié les occasions de porter atteinte aux intérêts propres à des opérateurs économiques limités en nombre et caractérisés souvent par des qualités très spécifiques. Même si la Cour s'est efforcée de tirer le meilleur parti possible des termes « clairement restrictifs » de l'alinéa 2 de l'article 173, les difficultés rencontrées par les requérants ont entraîné des « détournements de procédure » en direction du renvoi préjudiciel en appréciation de validité et du contentieux de l'indemnisation encore que, dans ce dernier cas, la Cour a formulé des exigences dont la rigueur n'a cessé de se renforcer. Aussi ne peut-on ignorer les propositions qui ont été faites *de lege ferenda* en vue d'améliorer la condition de ceux qu'on a coutume d'appeler les « requérants ordinaires » ou encore de manière plus révélatrice les requérants « non privilégiés ». D'ailleurs, la Cour a elle-même souhaité que « les actes de droit dérivé soient susceptibles de recours de la part des particuliers qui justifient d'un intérêt direct, comme il en est dans le système juridique de plusieurs Etats membres » ([49]). Peut-être conviendrait-il de systématiser et de prendre en compte la distinction des « règlements de base » et des « règlements d'exécution » née de la pratique et consacrée par la Cour de justice, pour envisager d'ouvrir aux particuliers, sans restric-

---

([48]) Voy. rapport de Lord Reay fait au nom de la commission politique du Parlement européen, 30 mai 1978, document 148/7, p. 40 et suiv., n° 79 et 80.

([49]) Contribution au rapport sur l'Union européenne, précitée, p. 38.

tion, le recours en annulation contre les seconds en limitant la portée des restrictions de l'alinéa 2 de l'article 173 aux seuls « règlements de base ». Ce serait, en somme, consacrer l'existence d'une hiérarchie correspondant quelque peu à la distinction du « législatif » et de l'« administratif ». Cette approche pourrait aussi contribuer à faciliter une participation accrue du Parlement européen à l'exercice du pouvoir législatif dans la Communauté. Une autre démarche consisterait à habiliter les particuliers « à introduire un recours direct auprès de la Cour de Justice contre un acte posé par une des institutions de l'Union qui violerait leurs droits fondamentaux » ([50]). Etroitement liée à la garantie des droits fondamentaux de l'individu dans la Communauté, elle supposerait que ceux-ci soient consignés dans un « catalogue » qui lui soit propre ou qu'elle adhère à la Convention européenne des droits de l'homme. Dans un cas comme dans l'autre, les perspectives sont très incertaines.

L'orientation donnée par la Cour à sa jurisprudence en matière de responsabilité extra-contractuelle de la Communauté suscite d'incontestables réserves. Si elle a, avec raison, affirmé l'autonomie du contentieux de l'indemnité par rapport à celui de la légalité, la rigueur des exigences auxquelles elle subordonne l'engagement de la responsabilité des institutions communautaires atteint un degré qui ne saurait être dépassé sans priver de toute protection les intéressés lorsque le préjudice a pour cause des « actes normatifs comportant des choix de politique économique » ([51]).

C) Le recours en constatation de manquement

La procédure en constatation de manquement a, elle aussi, ses limites puisque la Cour ne saurait annuler un acte national contraire au droit communautaire, même si les effets de ses arrêts dépassent ceux des arrêts purement déclaratoires, et surtout qu'ils sont prolongés par les obligations qui en résultent pour les juridictions nationales. Dans le souci de renforcer ses arrêts, la Cour, constatant que le traité de la CEE ne prévoit pas expressément de sanction effective en cas de manquement, a exprimé le souhait que « l'arrêt de manquement puisse préciser les mesures que l'Etat défaillant serait invité à prendre, d'autre part que l'exécution de cet arrêt soit placé sous un contrôle systématique approprié, et qu'enfin les avantages sollicités par l'Etat concerné soient liés à la régularisation du manquement ».

([50]) Rapport TINDEMANS, *Bull. CE*, supplément 1/76, p. 33.

([51]) Voy. en particulier l'arrêt *Bayerische HNL et autres c. Conseil et Commission*, 25 mai 1978, affaires jointes 83 et 94-76, 4, 15 et 40-77, *Rec.*, 1978, p. 1209 et suiv. et la note R. KOVAR au *Journal du Droit international*, 1978, p. 942 et suiv.

DISCUSSION

M. GOFFIN, *président*

Je vais non pas résumer l'exposé très dense du professeur Kovar, mais essayer de dégager de celui-ci certaines questions qui pourraient plus particulièrement retenir notre attention.

— Nous pourrions tout d'abord consacrer un échange de vues à la procédure préjudicielle de l'article 177 qui, ainsi que l'a montré l'arrêt *Van Gend en Loos,* organise une coopération judiciaire entre la Cour de justice et les juridictions nationales.

En ce qui concerne le recours en appréciation de validité, une des questions qui se posent — nous a rappelé le professeur Kovar — est de savoir s'il est acceptable que des juridictions nationales ne statuant pas en dernier ressort puissent déclarer invalide un acte communautaire. Pour ma part, je me rallie à l'excellente solution proposée par M. Bebr (1) : la juridiction qui estime que l'acte d'une institution de la Communauté n'est pas valide ne doit pas constater elle-même cette invalidité. Elle doit déférer la question à la Cour de justice.

En ce qui concerne le recours en interprétation, le professeur Kovar nous a dit, à juste titre, que la distinction entre interprétation et application est parfois assez délicate. La Cour de justice va très loin dans son interprétation qui constitue parfois une « préapplication ». Mais ce n'est pas là que réside la véritable difficulté.

Les problèmes les plus graves viennent de l'attitude des juridictions nationales qui refusent, soit de saisir la Cour de justice de questions préjudicielles, soit de reconnaître l'autorité de ses arrêts.

Le professeur Kovar a mentionné deux remèdes : recours direct des parties intéressées devant la Cour de justice, pourvoi dans l'intérêt de la loi.

Je me demande s'il n'y a pas un troisième remède qui vous semblera peut-être très audacieux puisqu'il va plus loin que l'arrêt *Simmenthal* qui, pouvait-on penser, avait déjà tiré les conséquences extrêmes des théories de l'effet direct et de la primauté. Ne peut-on admettre que l'exécution d'un arrêt coulé en force de chose jugée, contraire à un arrêt de la Cour de jus-

---

* NDLR. Dans le présent compte rendu, les questions et les réponses ont été regroupées par thème. L'ordre chronologique des interventions n'a donc pas été respecté.

(1) Examen en validité au titre de l'article 177 du traité CEE et cohésion juridique de la Communauté, *Cah. dr. eur.*, 1975, p. 379.

tice, soit refusée, en raison de la primauté du droit communautaire sur le droit national ? On pourrait également envisager la possibilité d'un recours en dommages-intérêts. Dans ce cas, les citoyens de la Communauté ne seraient pas placés sur un pied d'égalité puisque la législation permettant de mettre en cause le pouvoir judiciaire n'est pas la même dans les différents États membres. J'aimerais connaître l'opinion du professeur Kovar sur ces différents points.

— Nous pourrions, au cours de la seconde partie de cette discussion, centrer nos débats sur les trois aspects des compétences de la Cour de justice qui retiennent l'attention du professeur Kovar : contrôle de constitutionnalité, protection judiciaire des individus et constatation de manquement.

Le contrôle de constitutionnalité, tout d'abord. Le professeur Kovar estime que la Cour de justice devrait être compétente pour annuler un acte du Conseil européen, mais il s'est demandé si les conditions politiques actuelles permettaient l'exercice d'une telle compétence. A mon avis, lorsque le Conseil européen agit comme Conseil des ministres, la Cour de justice est compétente pour apprécier la validité de ses actes, sans que l'on ait à tenir compte de considérations d'ordre politique.

D'autre part, étant donné le texte restrictif de l'article 173 du traité de la CEE, est-il possible que le Parlement européen prenne l'initiative d'un recours contre un acte du Conseil ou de la Commission ? Est-il possible d'introduire un recours contre un acte du Parlement ? Je partage les hésitations du professeur Kovar à cet égard.

Que l'article 173 du traité de Rome fixe des conditions de recours trop restrictives pour permettre une protection judiciaire satisfaisante des particuliers est admis par tous. La distinction entre règlements de base et règlements d'exécution s'impose mais elle ne permet pas de résoudre le problème en ce qui concerne le recours en annulation. Elle permettrait peut-être à la Cour de justice d'infléchir sa jurisprudence dans un sens moins restrictif en ce qui concerne le recours en indemnité.

Quant à la constatation des manquements des États membres, le professeur Kovar proposait que les arrêts de la Cour de justice précisent les mesures qui devraient être prises par les Etats membres pour se conformer au droit communautaire. Cette suggestion est-elle suffisante ?

Voilà, brièvement résumées, les différentes questions que je vous propose d'examiner...

I. LES RECOURS PREJUDICIELS EN APPRECIATION DE VALIDITE ET EN INTERPRETATION

M. DRUESNE

De nombreux auteurs s'accordent pour critiquer le fait que les juges nationaux de première instance ont la faculté de se prononcer sur la validité d'un acte communautaire.

On pourrait envisager une solution maximaliste imposant aux juridictions de première instance — et non plus seulement aux juridictions suprêmes — de saisir la Cour de justice dès que se pose une question d'appréciation de validité d'une norme de droit communautaire.

L'efficacité d'une telle solution serait toutefois atténuée en raison de la possibilité qu'ont les juges d'appel dans tous nos systèmes juridiques, de censurer la décision de première instance.

Le problème est le même pour le recours en interprétation. Pour ce qui est de ce dernier, on peut trouver un exemple de cette difficulté dans un arrêt bien connu : l'arrêt *Cohn-Bendit* rendu par le Conseil d'Etat de France au mois de décembre 1978. M. Cohn-Bendit avait introduit, devant le tribunal administratif de Paris, un recours tendant à l'annulation de la décision du ministre français de l'Intérieur refusant d'abroger un arrêté d'expulsion pris à son encontre en 1968. M. Cohn-Bendit invoquait, à l'appui de son recours en annulation de l'acte individuel le concernant, la violation par l'administration française d'une disposition de la directive du Conseil de la Communauté économique européenne du 25 février 1964 (n° 64/221) relative à la coordination des mesures spéciales aux étrangers en matière de déplacement et de séjour justifiées par des raisons d'ordre public, de sécurité publique et de santé publique. Le tribunal de Paris, estimant que se posaient des questions d'interprétation de ladite directive, saisit la Cour de justice des Communautés à titre préjudiciel. Le ministre français de l'Intérieur fit appel contre le jugement de renvoi. Le Conseil d'Etat de France a considéré qu'il n'y avait pas lieu de saisir la Cour de justice et a annulé le jugement de renvoi du tribunal administratif de Paris.

Dans son arrêt, le Conseil d'Etat a estimé que l'article 189 du traité de Rome est libellé de telle manière que seuls les règlements peuvent avoir des effets directs, et non les directives, et il invoque à nouveau la fameuse théorie de l'acte clair pour justifier le refus de saisine de la Cour.

Je ne me livrerai pas ici à une étude approfondie de l'arrêt du Conseil d'Etat d'autant plus que sur le fond, le mécanisme de protection des droits des justiciables qui en résulte offre des garanties presque équivalentes à celles résultant de la reconnaissance, par le juge communautaire, du bénéfice de l'applicabilité directe à la directive 64/221. Je ferai simplement observer qu'en agissant ainsi le Conseil d'Etat a tout de même interprété l'article 189 et qu'il avait peut-être l'obligation, en tant que juridiction suprême, de surseoir à statuer et de saisir lui-même la Cour de justice, comme le suggérait d'ailleurs le commissaire du gouvernement, soucieux du bon fonctionnement de la coopération entre la Cour et les juridictions nationales.

Mr JACOBS

I would just like to comment on that particular point.

The provisions of Article 177 of course at present give a lower court a discretion whether to refer and impose an obligation only on final courts. Personally, it seems to me inconceivable that there should be an obligation on lower courts to refer every question of Community law; the result would be to overwhelm the European Court.

There is a related question which has just been mentioned: whether there should be an appeal against the exercise of this discretion by the lower court. Personally I don't think that the existence of that appeal gives rise to many difficulties. The Cohn-Bendit case is perhaps an unfortunate example, but one can think of few examples in the Member States where such an appeal has regularly been exercised; certainly in the United Kingdom, so far as I know, there has almost never been an appeal against a decision either to refer or not to refer.

One last point was suggested to me by Professor Kovar's remarks. Professor Kovar like Dr Bebr has said that it is undesirable that a lower court should have the possibility of pronouncing a Community measure invalid. But listening to Professor Kovar's remarks this morning, I wonder whether that is in fact a correct interpretation of Article 177.

Could it not be said that Article 177 gives the lower courts the possibility of referring a question of validity to the European Court, but it doesn't necessarily follow from that that a lower national court can itself pronounce a Community measure invalid. That seems to me a rather literal approach of a kind one might expect from an English court. I don't think it is necessarily an appropriate interpretation of the Treaty and therefore I would suggest that a lower court of a Member State has the possibility of referring a question of validity but if it does not refer cannot itself pronounce the measure invalid. Therefore I would say in practice the lower court has a choice: either ot accept the validity of the measure or to refer the question of validity to the European Court.

M. PUISSOCHET

Dans son rapport, le professeur Kovar s'est référé implicitement à certains arrêts récents comme l'arrêt *Cohn-Bendit* et a essayé de trouver des remèdes aux problèmes qui surgissent lorsqu'une juridiction ignore, consciemment ou inconsciemment, l'obligation de renvoyer à la Cour de justice une question pour examen préjudiciel. C'est ainsi qu'il a évoqué les recours directs de l'intéressé et le pourvoi dans l'intérêt de la loi.

Je n'examinerai pas ici si le Conseil d'Etat de France a fait une application correcte de la théorie de l'acte clair dans l'arrêt *Cohn-Bendit*.

Je voudrais simplement insister sur le fait que le mécanisme de l'article 177 est un mécanisme de collaboration judiciaire qui, dans l'ensemble, a bien fonctionné. Le mieux peut être l'ennemi du bien. L'atmosphère actuelle, qui est une atmosphère de collaboration judiciaire, pourrait se transformer en atmosphère de défiance. Plutôt que de rechercher des moyens contraignants et difficiles à mettre en œuvre — on l'a reconnu —, il faut faire appel à la notion de confiance mutuelle, au développement des choses dans le temps. On obtiendra ainsi, je crois, de bien meilleurs résultats qu'en instaurant un système de surveillance, d'institutionnalisation de la méfiance.

M. LAGRANGE

En tant que conseiller d'Etat, je suis entièrement d'accord avec l'intervention de mon collègue, M. Puissochet. La confiance qui s'est instaurée entre les juridictions nationales et la Cour de justice est extrêmement précieuse.

Pour ma part, j'ai toujours essayé de concilier la théorie de l'acte clair avec les nécessités de l'article 177.

Selon la théorie de l'acte clair, lorsqu'il y a doute, le juge national doit saisir la Cour de justice. Lorsqu'il n'y a pas doute, il y a application et non pas interprétation et le juge national est compétent. C'est le cas notamment lorsque la juridiction chargée de l'interprétation a déjà interprété la disposition en cause.

Mais le Conseil d'Etat de France — il faut le reconnaître — tourne maintenant le dos à la théorie de l'acte clair. L'interprétation de l'article 189 du traité que le Conseil d'Etat considère comme évidente (la directive n'est pas d'application directe) ne coïncide pas du tout avec celle de la Cour de justice. Dans ce cas, la solution raisonnable est celle qui, dans l'affaire Cohn-Bendit, avait été proposée par le commissaire du gouvernement. Tout en partageant l'interprétation donnée à l'article 189 par le Conseil d'Etat, le commissaire du gouvernement a estimé que le devoir de celui-ci était de renvoyer l'affaire à la Cour de justice. Il souhaitait que cette dernière, interrogée à nouveau par une haute juridiction sur un point qu'elle avait tranché, accepte d'infléchir sa jurisprudence. Il y aurait alors eu une nouvelle manifestation de cette collaboration indispensable entre les juges nationaux et la Cour de justice.

M. KOVAR

A l'exception de l'une ou l'autre d'entre elles, la plupart des suggestions dont j'ai fait état ne sont pas de mon fait. Cette observation n'est pas destinée à dégager ma responsabilité ; j'ai cru devoir interpréter le mandat qui m'avait été donné en essayant aussi de recenser l'ensemble des propositions émanant d'institutions communautaires y compris de la Cour de justice. C'est ainsi que l'idée d'un pourvoi dans l'intérêt de la loi n'est pas d'origine purement doctrinale. Sans vouloir donc aucunement récuser les observations qui ont été faites, je tenais à rappeler ces circonstances.

Pour le reste, j'ai été surtout frappé par l'intérêt porté à la procédure du renvoi préjudiciel, peut-être encore plus d'ailleurs au renvoi préjudiciel en interprétation qu'au renvoi en appréciation de validité.

S'agissant du renvoi préjudiciel en appréciation de validité, pour mettre fin à toute ambiguïté, car j'ai eu le sentiment à un moment donné qu'on glissait de ce renvoi à son frère jumeau, je tiens à exprimer aussi clairement que je l'ai fait par écrit mon entière adhésion à l'interprétation qui a été donnée par M. Bebr, il y a quelques années, dans un article paru aux *Cahiers de droit européen* ([2]), sur la façon d'entendre les dispositions de l'article 177 concernant le renvoi préjudiciel en appréciation de validité. Autrement dit, les juridictions qui statuent en dernier ressort ont le choix entre constater la validité ou, si elles ont un doute, saisir la Cour de justice. Telle est en substance la conclusion à laquelle était parvenu M. Bebr au terme d'un raisonnement qui ne peut être restitué ici.

En ce qui concerne le renvoi préjudiciel en interprétation, je crois avoir dit très clairement qu'il était évident que toutes les propositions faites — pourvoi dans l'intérêt de la loi, éventuellement recours en appel (en réalité, ce ne saurait être au sens précis du terme un appel, mais telle est la formule utilisée dans les documents auxquels je fais allusion) — sont, en dépit de leurs mérites, pratiquement pour ne pas dire politiquement impraticables. A supposer même que les conditions de leur mise en œuvre soient réunies, l'insertion de pareilles procédures aurait pour effet de modifier profondément la nature des rapports qu'on a voulu établir entre la Cour de justice et les juridictions nationales.

([2]) Cité *supra*, note (1).

Mon collègue Druesne a amplement évoqué l'arrêt *Cohn-Bendit.* Ses observations n'appellent de ma part aucun commentaire. Aussi mon intention est de me borner à revenir sur la question de savoir si, effectivement, un juge national qui aurait décidé de saisir la Cour de justice d'une question préjudicielle ne risque pas d'en être ensuite empêché par un recours intenté contre la décision de renvoi. Je voudrais à cet égard faire deux observations.

D'abord, l'affaire *BRT c. Sabam* (3) et les affaires *Rheinmühlen* (4) ont donné lieu, au début de l'année 1974, à un échange de vues entre les avocats généraux, M. Warner et M. Mayras, à propos de la question de savoir si un appel pouvait être intenté contre la décision d'une juridiction saisissant la Cour de justice. Dans l'affaire *Rheinmühlen,* M. Warner avait conclu que l'appel n'était pas possible. Dans l'affaire *BRT c. Sabam,* M. Mayras avait estimé que l'exercice des voies de recours contre les décisions de renvoi des juridictions nationales n'était pas exclu de plein droit.

La Cour de justice a rendu une sorte de jugement de Salomon. Dans l'arrêt *BRT c. Sabam,* elle indique que la procédure devant la Cour de justice se poursuit tant que la demande du juge national n'a été ni retirée, ni mise à néant.

Dans l'affaire *Rheinmühlen,* une autre question avait été également posée. Il s'agissait de déterminer si une juridiction ne statuant pas en dernier ressort conservait la faculté de renvoyer à la Cour de justice lorsqu'elle est amenée à se prononcer une seconde fois sur l'affaire à la suite de l'annulation de son jugement ou si elle était liée par l'appréciation portée en droit par la juridiction du degré supérieur. La Cour de justice a estimé, dans le premier arrêt *Rheinmühlen,* que la juridiction avait le droit de saisir la Cour de justice, nonobstant la décision contraire de la juridiction supérieure, en l'occurrence la Cour fiscale suprême de la République fédérale d'Allemagne.

Pour en revenir à l'affaire *Cohn-Bendit,* il me semble que le tribunal administratif de Paris aurait pu saisir une seconde fois la Cour de justice, malgré l'arrêt du Conseil d'Etat, d'autant plus que le recours du ministre de l'Intérieur ne portait pas sur la question de l'effet direct de la directive du 25 février 1964. C'est le Conseil d'Etat qui, d'office, a examiné cette question.

---

(3) Aff. n° 127-73, *Belgische Radio en Televisie et Société belge des auteurs, compositeurs et éditeurs c. S.V. Sabam et N.V. Fonior* (demande de décision préjudicielle formée par le tribunal de première instance de Bruxelles), arrêt du 30 janvier 1974, *Rec.*, 1974, p. 51 et suiv.

(4) Affaire 166-73, *Rheinmühlen, Düsseldorf c. Einfuhr und Vorratsstelle für Getreide und Futtermittel* (demande de décision préjudicielle, formée par le Bundesfinanzhof), arrêt du 16 janvier 1974, *Rec.*, 1974, p. 33 et suiv.
Affaire n° 146-73, mêmes parties au litige principal (demande de décision préjudicielle formée par le Hessisches Finanzgericht), arrêt du 12 février 1974, *Rec.*, 1974, p. 139 et suiv.

Telles sont les observations que je voulais faire à propos de la procédure de l'article 177. Pour terminer, je dirai qu'il est évident que l'esprit de collaboration souhaité par tous prévaut. La procédure de l'article 177 a fait ses preuves.

II. LES COMPETENCES DE LA COUR DE JUSTICE

1) Le contrôle de constitutionnalité

M. DEWOST

La question de l'assujettissement du Conseil européen au contrôle juridictionnel est un faux problème en raison tant de la nature du Conseil européen que de son mode de fonctionnement.

Le Conseil européen est une institution *sui generis* qui agit en réalité en tant que Conseil des Communautés lorsqu'il traite de questions relevant des traités, comme l'a dit le Conseil dans des réponses à des questions parlementaires.

Le Conseil européen fonctionne de plus en plus de la même manière que le Conseil des Communautés, c'est-à-dire en deux temps. Pour des raisons tenant à la complexité de ses ordres du jour et au temps limité dont disposent les ministres, 90 à 95 % des décisions du Conseil sont prises en deux étapes. Dans un premier temps, le Conseil examine le dossier, délibère et parvient à un accord politique. Dans un second temps, l'acte juridique (règlement ou directive) correspondant à la décision politique est adopté, suivant les circonstances, quelques jours ou quelques semaines plus tard, sous point A de l'ordre du jour du Conseil.

Le Conseil européen prend des décisions politiques qui sont concrétisées par des actes juridiques adoptés par un Conseil au niveau ministériel. Ceux-ci sont parfaitement susceptibles de faire l'objet d'un recours devant la Cour de justice. Il n'y a donc pas de problème spécifique au Conseil européen.

2) Les arrêts de constatation de manquement

M. PESCATORE

Le professeur Kovar a abordé la question de savoir si les arrêts en constatation de manquement pourraient avoir un caractère plus constructif, c'est-à-dire si la Cour de justice pourrait non seulement constater qu'il y a un manquement, mais aussi indiquer les mesures que l'Etat membre doit prendre pour se mettre en règle avec les exigences du droit communautaire.

C'est, comme vous le savez, un problème très actuel. Il existe au moins deux décisions de la Cour de justice qui permettent en principe de donner une réponse affirmative.

La première affaire était un recours en manquement d'Etat dirigé contre l'Allemagne en raison d'aides accordées à des charbonnages. Dans sa requête introductive, la Commission avait demandé à la Cour, d'une part, de constater l'illégalité de l'aide et, d'autre part, d'enjoindre au gouvernement allemand de récupérer les aides illégalement accordées. Dans son arrêt, la Cour a admis la recevabilité de la seconde requête de la Commission alors que celle-ci était contestée par le gouvernement allemand qui en avait fait une question préalable ([5]).

La deuxième affaire est un recours en constatation de manquement contre l'Irlande (affaire des pêcheries). Comme la Commission le lui avait demandé, la Cour a enjoint à l'Irlande, à titre de mesure provisoire, de suspendre immédiatement la mesure qui faisait l'objet de la contestation ([6]).

Par ailleurs, je voudrais citer encore un arrêt en constatation de manquement qui montre que la Cour a une conception large de la responsabilité des Etats membres du fait de leurs engagements communautaires.

Il s'agissait d'un recours en manquement d'Etat formé contre la République italienne qui n'avait pas exécuté convenablement un règlement du Conseil concernant l'abattage des vaches. L'Italie qui, au cours de la procédure, avait pris des mesures pour se mettre en conformité avec ledit règlement, plaidait devant la Cour l'irrecevabilité du recours. Dans son arrêt, la Cour a souligné que la constatation, même rétrospective, d'un manquement avait de l'intérêt, notamment parce qu'elle pouvait constituer la base d'une responsabilité de l'Etat membre à l'égard de la Communauté, d'autres Etats membres et de particuliers ([7]).

M. BARAV

Je voudrais faire quelques remarques à propos des arrêts en constatation de manquement cités par M. Pescatore.

Dans l'affaire des mines allemandes, la Commission avait demandé à la Cour d'ordonner des mesures concrètes. La Cour a répondu de manière

(5) Arrêt du 12 juillet 1973, aff. 70-72, *Rec.*, 1973, p. 813.
(6) Ordonnance du 22 mai 1977, aff. 61-77, *Rec.*, 1977, p. 937.
(7) Arrêt du 7 février 1972, aff. 39-72, *Rec.*, 1972, p. 112.

ambiguë. Elle n'indique pas clairement si elle se reconnaît la possibilité d'indiquer *ex officio,* en l'absence de demande de la Commission, les mesures que l'Etat devrait prendre.

La même observation vaut pour les mesures conservatoires ordonnées dans l'affaire irlandaise des pêcheries. Dans une affaire britannique du même jour, l'avocat général avait estimé que la Cour n'était pas compétente pour ordonner des mesures conservatoires.

J'aimerais que M. Pescatore nous dise si la Cour de justice s'estime compétente pour indiquer aux Etats membres les mesures à prendre, sans qu'il y ait une requête de la Commission.

M. RYZIGER

Il est vrai que la confiance est à la base des rapports entre les juridictions nationales et la Cour de justice. Les résistances qui se manifestent, en particulier au Conseil d'Etat, sont sans doute la manifestation de conflits de générations qui peuvent encore jouer à l'heure actuelle.

Il n'en reste pas moins qu'il serait absolument intolérable que le refus d'appliquer les normes communautaires se concrétise par une résistance à la jurisprudence de la Cour de justice, et qu'il se développe. Au lieu d'une interprétation unique du droit communautaire par la Cour de justice, on se trouverait en présence, comme c'est le cas pour les traités classiques — je pense, par exemple, aux conventions sur la compétence judiciaire —, d'interprétations jurisprudentielles différentes dans les divers Etats signataires du traité de Rome.

Il est donc indispensable de trouver des remèdes pour que l'échafaudage communautaire ne s'écroule pas. Le professeur Kovar a proposé deux solutions *de lege ferenda.* Mais, comme M. Pescatore nous le disait tout à l'heure, il paraît hors de question, dans le climat politique actuel, de « renégocier » le traité de Rome dans une optique supranationale.

Le professeur Goffin a proposé une troisième solution qui me paraît difficile à mettre en œuvre. Au surplus, dans certains systèmes — c'est le cas du système juridictionnel français notamment — la responsabilité de l'Etat, en raison d'une faute juridictionnelle, est absolument inconcevable en l'état actuel du droit.

Une quatrième voie serait peut-être de recourir à l'article 169 du traité de Rome. Certes, cette solution présente des difficultés, et n'est pas sans inconvénients.

Au premier abord, on voit mal ce qu'un Etat pourrait faire pour vaincre la résistance d'une juridiction qui méconnaîtrait le droit communautaire.

L'histoire nous fournit, cependant, des enseignements dont on pourrait s'inspirer. C'est ainsi qu'en France, à plusieurs reprises, la Cour de Cassation a été obligée de modifier l'interprétation qu'elle avait donnée de certaines lois à la suite de l'adoption, dans ce but, de lois interprétatives par le Parlement. Il existe donc, en France au moins, la possibilité de vaincre, pour l'avenir, une résistance juridictionnelle par l'adoption d'une législation *ad hoc.*

Si on donne une interprétation exégétique du traité, rien ne permet de dire qu'un refus par une juridiction d'appliquer une norme communautaire doive échapper au jeu de l'article 169. Il en est d'autant plus ainsi que l'autorité judiciaire a des fonctions juridiques moins nettement différenciées des autres pouvoirs qu'on ne le croit souvent.

Techniquement, le pouvoir judiciaire n'a qu'une fonction exécutive, à telle enseigne que certains considèrent qu'ayant pour mission d'appliquer les lois, il ne constitue qu'une branche de l'exécutif — une branche indépendante, certes, mais une branche tout de même. L'indépendance des tribunaux ne constitue pas un argument suffisant pour évincer le jeu de l'article 169. Dans l'affaire de l'arrachage des arbres fruitiers italiens, la Cour de justice a déclaré expressément qu'un Etat était responsable de l'action de son Parlement sur lequel le gouvernement n'avait, cependant, pas de prise. Cette jurisprudence peut également s'appliquer aux juridictions.

Il est vrai que le recours à l'article 169 présenterait plusieurs inconvénients lorsqu'une résistance juridictionnelle s'est manifestée.

Tout d'abord, c'est essentiellement à la Commission qu'incomberait la charge d'introduire le recours. Or la Commission est un organe politique. Il serait certainement préférable que l'initiative du recours soit prise par un magistrat ; on pourrait penser au parquet général de la Cour de justice (si on peut parler de parquet général pour viser la collectivité des avocats généraux de la Cour de justice), au premier avocat général, par exemple, mais on retombe ici sur la nécessité de modifier le traité, à écarter par hypothèse.

Le second inconvénient serait de conforter les juges nationaux dans leur résistance.

Enfin, troisième inconvénient, comme il n'existe pas d'autres moyens techniques qu'une loi pour briser la résistance d'une juridiction suprême, on risquerait d'arriver à une responsabilité internationale diluée dans le cas où le Parlement national concerné refuserait de la voter.

Les arrêts de la Cour de justice, qui ont pourtant pour objectif de renforcer le système communautaire, finiraient par ressembler aux arrêts de la Cour internationale de justice et par dire le droit à une hauteur telle qu'ils seraient inapplicables.

M. Hjalte RASMUSSEN

I would like to point to one important factor which we quite consciously, I suppose, have omitted from the focus of our discussions to-day, but which nevertheless in my view deserves to be expressly mentioned.

From studying the Court's case reports one readily notices that the preliminary procedure under Article 177 takes up the major working time of the Court; up to 75 or 80% of the cases are references under Article 177.

This bias has created certains problems for the Court. In the first place are well known the difficulties for the Court, in all cases, to know precisely which are the relevant constitutional facts of the case and which are the relevant constitutional, social and political consequences of the decisions. Without a comprehensive factual, in this wide sense, knowledge any attempt to judicial policy-making becomes a policy-making in the blind—if part of the policy-making in fact is not inadvertently accomplished. The member states are obviously trying to remedy this situation by claiming a more permanent and direct access to the Court's case-handling, as Francis Jacobs has pointed out for us.

The discussion about the Court's policy-making necessarily comes to be biased by this fact. I believe that it will be important, in the years to come, to see if the Commission would not use more widely the procedure under Article 169.

Hopefully, there are signs, which already are noticeable in the case-reports of the Court, that the Commission is initiating more cases of this type. This is, for the purpose of the discussion of any judicial policy-making, a happy development that deserves to be underlined.

This development is important because the member states, in the Article 169-procedures are given the opportunity to defend themselves; not only the "incriminated" member state but also member states intervening in a case could thoroughly analyse and discuss the policy implications of the one or the other judicial solution of the case. For the most part only the member states have the ability and dispose of the resources necessary for producing what the Americans call a "Brandeis brief", i.e. briefly, an exhaustive verification and analysis of the relevant constitutional fact and the decisions policy-alternatives and consequences.

M. PAULIN

Mes observations portent également sur l'intervention que M. le juge Pescatore a faite au sujet de l'exécution des arrêts de la Cour.

Elles concernent un problème tout à fait théorique et non pas un exemple concret que tout le monde peut avoir à l'esprit.

Dans l'arrêt constatant le manquement de l'Italie dans l'affaire de l'abattage des vaches, nous a rappelé M. Pescatore, la Cour de justice a dit qu'en n'exécutant pas un arrêt de la Cour, un Etat membre engageait sa responsabilité vis-à-vis des institutions, des particuliers et des autres Etats membres.

La responsabilité à l'égard des particuliers ne pose pas de problème. Les particuliers se retournent, contre l'Etat qui a commis le manquement, devant les tribunaux nationaux de cet Etat.

Pour la responsabilité à l'égard des autres Etats membres, il faudrait admettre que, si un Etat membre ne respecte par un arrêt de la Cour constatant le manquement, les autres Etats membres qui s'estiment lésés par cette attitude puissent introduire un deuxième recours devant la Cour. Je me demande comment il faudrait bâtir ce recours pour qu'il aboutisse au paiement d'une indemnité — cas qui n'est pas prévu par le traité. Il devrait probablement s'agir d'un recours en vertu de l'article 170 et ce recours devrait sans doute être fondé sur la violation, par l'Etat membre qui n'a pas respecté l'arrêt de la Cour, d'une obligation sous-jacente au traité : celle de réparer les dommages qu'il a pu causer.

M. KOVAR

Si, dans l'ensemble, la procédure préjudicielle a fonctionné de manière satisfaisante, il reste que — M. Ryziger l'a très bien souligné —, sans être excessivement pessimiste, on ne saurait exclure la multiplication des cas de rebellion de juridictions nationales refusant délibérément certaines conséquences des arrêts de la Cour de justice. Il serait vain de penser que l'arrêt *Cohn-Bendit* du Conseil d'Etat de France est et demeure un cas isolé. D'autres juridictions non moins éminentes, dont les cours constitutionnelles, se sont plus ou moins nettement opposées à la Cour de justice des Communautés. Ces situations sont donc bien réelles.

Dans mon rapport écrit, je me suis expliqué à propos de la procédure de l'article 169 du traité de la CEE. J'ai constaté que la Commission elle-même, interrogée à plusieurs reprises sur ce point, avait estimé qu'aucune raison de principe ne permettait d'exclure l'application de cette procédure en raison de ce que le manquement était le fait d'une juridiction. Effectivement, les considérations exposées par M. Ryziger doivent être retenues. La Cour de justice avait déjà tenu à souligner que la nature de l'institution fautive est indifférente. L'application de ce principe à un organe parlementaire étant certaine, rien n'autorise à considérer que les juridictions, voire même les juridictions suprêmes, doivent y échapper.

Reste qu'il faut tout de même exécuter l'arrêt rendu par la Cour, spécialement lorsque toutes les voies de droit ordinaires et extraordinaires permettant une remise en cause du jugement constitutif d'un manquement sont épuisées.

L'intervention législative ne me paraît pas être une excellente solution puisqu'elle se réalise nécessairement au détriment de l'indépendance des juridictions. Néanmoins, il est des circonstances où elle s'avère absolument nécessaire. C'est pourquoi on ne saurait exclure qu'il y soit fait exceptionnellement appel.

Toutefois, l'intervention législative pourrait trouver difficulté à se concilier avec les conséquences de l'effet direct du droit communautaire telles qu'elles ont été exprimées par la Cour en particulier dans ses arrêts 48-71, *Commission contre Italie* (8) et *Simmenthal* (9), sous la forme d'une obligation pour tout juge de prohiber de plein droit l'application de toute règle contraire à une norme communautaire. Certes, il convient d'être pragmatique. Pour autant, on ne saurait négliger la nécessité d'une cohérence logique avec les principes structurels de l'ordre juridique communautaire. Nous rejoignons par là une suggestion peut-être considérée comme « extrémiste » par d'aucuns. L'arrêt *Simmenthal* ne devrait pas être regardé comme le terme ultime des développements jurisprudentiels. Il conviendrait d'aller au-delà encore pour considérer que les autorités nationales autres que les juridictions — on observera d'ailleurs que, dans son arrêt 48-71, la Cour vise non seulement les juridictions mais plus généralement les autorités nationales — sont tenues de ne pas exécuter une décision de justice qui méconnaîtrait un arrêt de la Cour de justice. Pareille exigence ne manquerait évidemment d'embarrasser les autorités nationales prises dans le dilemme d'une double allégeance. Il est certain que nous touchons du doigt à l'un des problèmes essentiels, à savoir la conciliation entre le principe de l'autonomie institutionnelle appliqué aux organes judiciaires d'une part et l'exigence de plus en plus drastique de faire produire à la norme d'effet direct la plénitude de ses effets d'autre part.

Un autre aspect du problème pourrait aussi être évoqué. Les règles de procédure et notamment les règles fixant les délais de recours sont différentes d'un Etat à l'autre, ce qui ne permet pas une application uniforme du droit communautaire. Dans les arrêts *Comet* (10) et *Rewe* (11), la Cour a dû reconnaître que la théorie de l'effet direct ne permettait pas de trouver une

---

(8) Arrêt du 13 juillet 1972, *Rec.*, 1972, p. 529.
(9) Arrêt du 9 mars 1978, aff. n° 106-77, *Rec.*, 1978, p. 629.
(10) Arrêt du 16 décembre 1976, aff. n° 45-76, *Rec.*, 1976, p. 2043.
(11) Arrêt du 16 décembre 1976, aff. n° 53-76, *Rec.*, 1976, p. 1989.

solution satisfaisante au problème posé et que seule une harmonisation des règles procédurales fondée sur l'article 100 pourrait régler cette question.

Enfin, je voudrais dire quelques mots sur le problème des injonctions.

Je crois qu'on peut donner de l'arrêt rendu par la Cour de justice dans l'affaire des charbonnages allemands une interprétation un peu différente de celle proposée par M. le juge Pescatore. On peut considérer que la Cour n'a pas donné de véritables injonctions au gouvernement allemand mais a simplement estimé que, pour faire produire un effet utile à la disposition en cause — l'article 92 —, il était nécessaire que le gouvernement allemand obtienne la restitution des subventions qu'il avait accordées.

D'autre part, les injonctions données par la Cour dans le cadre de mesures conservatoires ont pour but d'éviter une aggravation du litige, précisément au moment où l'on cherche à le résoudre. On peut se demander si l'arrêt définitif rendu dans le cadre d'une procédure de manquement pourrait lui aussi comporter des injonctions. En tout cas, il est des auteurs qui en doutent.

LES ETATS MEMBRES ET LA JURISPRUDENCE DE LA COUR*

par

Jean-Victor LOUIS, Georges VANDERSANDEN
et Michel WAELBROECK,

Professeurs à l'Université libre de Bruxelles

Sauf des exceptions récentes, l'autorité de la Cour a été respectée jusqu'à présent par les Etats membres comme par les particuliers. Toutefois, les orientations de la jurisprudence ont souvent fait l'objet de critiques plus ou moins exprimées, dues à des malentendus sur le rôle et les méthodes d'interprétation de la Cour. Cette incompréhension se manifeste en particulier chez les juristes de *Common Law* depuis l'élargissement.

Le présent rapport a pour objet d'examiner, d'abord, les raisons de ces malentendus et de contribuer à désamorcer un débat qui tend à devenir de plus en plus politique.

Ensuite, il s'attachera à dégager le rôle de la jurisprudence dans l'évolution du processus d'intégration.

Il ne s'agit pas de présenter une étude plus ou moins exhaustive des techniques d'interprétation. Ce travail a déjà été fait en d'autres occasions (1). Le propos est plutôt d'introduire une discussion, fondée sur des éléments concrets tirés de la jurisprudence, en vue de cerner de plus près les ressorts de l'action de la Cour de justice et le rôle original mais difficile qui est le sien.

I. LA COUR, JUGE INTERNATIONAL OU JUGE CONSTITUTIONNEL ?

Le propos n'est pas de susciter une controverse théorique sur un sujet qui peut paraître usé, mais bien plutôt de mettre l'accent sur les tensions entre une vision internationale de l'ordre juridique communautaire et une vision constitutionnelle. Dans les traités coexistent des mécanismes qui relèvent de l'une et de l'autre conception. Un même recours peut faire l'objet d'interprétations divergentes selon qu'on se réfère plutôt à un schéma inter-

---

* Chacun des co-auteurs a présenté oralement une partie de leur rapport conjoint.

(1) Voy. *Rencontre judiciaire et universitaire des 27-28 septembre 1976*, organisée par la Cour de justice (Luxembourg, 1976).

nationaliste ou à une analyse de droit interne (exemple : recours en manquement). La jurisprudence a accentué ces tensions, notamment par l'importance attachée à l'effet direct.

On doit certes reconnaître que l'opposition entre une conception internationale de l'ordre juridique communautaire et la qualification de la Cour, comme une juridiction constitutionnelle, est assurément simplificatrice et forcée parce qu'il est parfois difficile, comme le révélera l'analyse, d'attribuer tel ou tel trait de la jurisprudence à l'une ou à l'autre de ces visions. Il en est ainsi, par exemple, du rôle de la pratique des Etats dans l'interprétation des traités-constitutions.

Toutefois, il paraît incontestable que c'est de la méconnaissance des finalités du rôle de la Cour que naissent les malentendus à propos de sa jurisprudence. Les Etats tendent toujours à privilégier le rôle international de la Cour et à faire prévaloir une interprétation restrictive et intergouvernementale des dispositions des traités. Cela a toujours été le cas, au point que les Etats n'ont pas hésité à proposer des interprétations dont le bienfondé pouvait paraître contestable même dans une optique strictement « internationaliste ». Il suffit de se souvenir de la prise de position souvent évoquée de trois Etats contre l'effet direct des dispositions du traité CEE dans la célèbre affaire *Van Gend en Loos*.

D'où l'intérêt d'une analyse plus systématique des tensions qui découlent des contradictions entre l'international et le fédéral qui sont typiques de l'ordre juridique communautaire.

A. L'IRREVERSIBILITE DU DESSAISISSEMENT DES ETATS

Les Etats membres, qui ont conservé leur personnalité juridique internationale et n'ont attribué à la Communauté que des compétences déterminées, répugnent à admettre le caractère irréversible du dessaisissement qui en résulte. Ayant le pouvoir du dernier mot dans la procédure de revision des traités, dirigeant la Communauté par leurs représentants au Conseil, ils revendiquent l'omnipotence en dépit des limitations d'action que comportent les traités.

La Cour, en tant qu'institution chargée d'assurer le respect du droit dans l'interprétation et l'application des traités, assure le maintien de la règle à l'encontre de la prétention des Etats à faire triompher l'expression de leur volonté politique sur les règles des traités.

Elle réagit en termes de limitation de souveraineté aux arguments fondés sur la désuétude d'un régime communautaire et sur le retour aux Etats des compétences conférées comme suite à leur non usage.

C'est tout le problème du conflit sur l'application du chapitre VI du traité Euratom (voy. arrêt du 14 décembre 1971 (2) et délibération n° 1-78 (3)).

De même, la Cour refuse toute portée juridique obligatoire aux résolutions des représentants des gouvernements ou du Conseil reportant la date d'application de dispositions du traité (article 119, arrêt *Defrenne II* (4) et article 37, arrêt *Manghera* (5)).

La règle générale d'interprétation énoncée à l'article 31, paragraphe 3 de la convention de Vienne sur le droit des traités selon laquelle il sera tenu compte, en même temps que du contexte, de tout accord ultérieur intervenu entre les parties au sujet de l'interprétation d'un traité ou de l'application de ses dispositions ainsi que du rôle de la pratique suivie dans cette application n'a qu'une portée limitée au sein de l'ordre juridique communautaire en raison du caractère rigide de sa constitution et de sa structure très légaliste.

C'est dans le même esprit que, faisant application du principe de confiance légitime et de la règle *patere legem quam ipse fecisti,* la Cour donne effet à des résolutions auxquelles le Conseil aurait voulu conserver un caractère politique (arrêt du 5 juin 1973, aff. n° 81-72, *Commission c. Conseil* (6)). Déjà, dans son arrêt *AETR,* la Cour avait reconnu le caractère d'une décision obligatoire à une mesure de coordination des positions des Etats membres dans la négociation de l'accord à conclure au sein de la Commission économique pour l'Europe des Nations unies (7).

Le recours du Conseil et du Conseil européen à des actes innommés, plutôt qu'aux catégories d'actes dont l'article 189 du traité CEE définit la portée, est révélateur des tentatives faites par les gouvernements pour échapper au carcan de contraintes juridiques dans des domaines où ils veulent conserver leur liberté d'action (8).

Faute de considérer de tels actes comme partie intégrante du bloc de la légalité communautaire, la Cour risquerait de voir celui-ci vidé d'une part essentielle de sa substance et, dès lors, son rôle de gardienne de cette légalité serait entamé.

---

(2) Aff. n° 7-71, arrêt du 14 décembre 1971, *Commission c. France, Rec.*, 1971, p. 1003 et suiv.
(3) *Rec.*, 1978, p. 2151 et suiv.
(4) Aff. n° 43-75, arrêt du 8 avril 1976, *Rec.*, 1976, p. 455.
(5) Aff. n° 59-75, arrêt du 3 février 1976, *Rec.*, 1976, p. 91 et suiv.
(6) *Rec.*, 1973, p. 575 et suiv.
(7) Aff. n° 22-70, arrêt du 31 mars 1971, *Rec.*, 1971, p. 263 et suiv.
(8) La Cour a eu à connaître des effets juridiques d'une résolution du Conseil et des représentants des gouvernements des Etats membres en matière monétaire dans l'affaire *Schlüter*, n° 9-73, 24 octobre 1973, *Rec.*, 1973, p. 1135; elle a relevé en l'espèce le caractère essentiellement politique de cette résolution.

Au refus des Etats de se considérer liés juridiquement par l'expression de leur volonté, la Cour oppose le caractère fortement « juridicisé » de l'ordre dont elle est l'un des piliers. En revanche, elle refuse la sanction juridique à des accords contraires aux exigences constitutionnelles communautaires.

Il ne peut être dénié que, par cette attitude, la Cour se comporte pleinement comme un organe juridictionnel. Etant — au même titre que le Conseil, la Commission et le Parlement — une « institution » de la Communauté (article 4), elle faillirait au rôle qui lui a été assigné par le traité si elle ne veillait pas au maintien de l'intégrité du cadre juridique dans lequel la Communauté est appelée à poursuivre son action et si elle ne s'opposait pas aux velléités manifestées par les Etats membres de se ressaisir des compétences attribuées à la Communauté.

B. LE CARACTERE EVOLUTIF DE LA JURISPRUDENCE DE LA COUR

On oppose souvent le principe de l'interprétation restrictive des traités internationaux traditionnels à celui de l'interprétation « finaliste » ou « téléologique » des traités communautaires. Cette opposition est en grande mesure exagérée, dans la mesure où les juridictions internationales elles-mêmes tiennent compte dans l'interprétation des traités instituant une organisation internationale des objectifs et des finalités de celle-ci, allant même jusqu'à reconnaître à l'organisation des « pouvoirs implicites » (avis consultatif de la Cour internationale de justice du 11 avril 1949 relatif à la réparation des dommages subis au service des Nations Unies ([9])).

Toujours est-il que cette opposition a contribué à encourager les critiques de certains à l'égard du caractère évolutif et « finaliste » de la jurisprudence de la Cour de justice.

Le développement de cette jurisprudence s'est fait de manière progressive, franchissant les obstacles un à un et s'enhardissant au fur et à mesure des progrès accomplis. Cette démarche fut favorisée par l'absence de travaux préparatoires officiellement publiés — qui auraient pu freiner l'évolution jurisprudentielle en « cristallisant » les interprétations voulues par les auteurs des traités. La lourdeur des mécanismes législatifs a, de son côté, incité la Cour à ne pas s'en tenir à une interprétation littérale des textes mais à accorder une importance déterminante aux objectifs poursuivis.

([9]) *Recueil des arrêts, avis consultatifs et ordonnances de la Cour internationale de justice*, 1949, p. 174.

On en donnera quelques exemples :

1) **Extension donnée au champ d'application territoriale du traité**

Dans l'arrêt *Bozzone* ([10]), la Cour étend le principe de non-discrimination en matière de sécurité sociale aux travailleurs de nationalité communautaire ayant exercé leurs activités dans les anciennes colonies.

De même, l'arrêt *Hansen* du 10 octobre 1978 ([11]) considère que l'expiration du délai de deux ans prévu à l'article 227, paragraphe 2, a entraîné l'application de plein droit aux départements français d'outre-mer de toutes les dispositions du traité.

Cette décision paraît audacieuse, si l'on tient compte de ce que le texte du traité disposait que les conditions d'application de l'article 95 aux départements d'outre-mer devaient être déterminées par le Conseil au plus tard deux ans après l'entrée en vigueur du traité. Il paraissait logique d'en déduire, comme l'avaient fait le Conseil et la Commission, de même que la doctrine, qu'à défaut de décision du Conseil fixant ces conditions d'application l'article 95 demeurait inapplicable aux départements d'outre-mer.

2) **Extension donnée au champ d'application matériel de certaines dispositions**

a) *Taxes d'effet équivalent*

L'arrêt *Sociaal Fonds voor de Dimantarbeiders* ([12]) décide que l'interdiction de l'article 12 s'applique à toute taxe frappant exclusivement les produits importés, même si cette taxe n'a aucun effet protecteur, en l'absence de toute production nationale.

Selon l'arrêt *Rewe-Zentrale* ([13]), l'interdiction s'applique même aux taxes rémunératoires d'un service rendu (en l'espèce une inspection phytosanitaire), du moment que l'importateur (ou l'exportateur) n'est pas libre de renoncer au service en cause.

Les arrêts *Capolongo* ([14]), *IGAV* ([15]) et *Cucchi* ([16]) considèrent (contrairement à la jurisprudence antérieure qui avait toujours nettement distingué

([10]) Arrêt du 31 mars 1977, aff. n° 87-76, *Rec.*, 1977, p. 687.

([11]) Aff. n° 148-77, *Rec.*, 1978, p. 1787.

([12]) Arrêt du 1er juillet 1969, aff. jtes n°s 2 et 3-69, *Rec.*, 1969, p. 211.

([13]) Arrêt du 11 octobre 1973, aff. n° 39-73, *Rec.*, 1973, p. 1039.

([14]) Arrêt du 19 juin 1973, aff. n° 77-72, *Rec.*, 1973, p. 611.

([15]) Arrêt du 18 juin 1975, aff. n° 94-74, *Rec.*, 1975, p. 699.

([16]) Arrêt du 25 mai 1977, n° 77-76, *Rec.*, 1977, p. 987.

entre taxes frappant exclusivement des produits importés et taxes intérieures frappant tant les produits nationaux que les produits importés) que l'interdiction s'étend aux charges qui visent tant les produits nationaux que les produits importés selon les mêmes critères, du moment que leur produit est utilisé pour financer des activités qui bénéficient de façon spécifique au produit national taxé, qu'il y a identité entre le produit taxé et le produit national bénéficiaire et que les charges pesant sur le produit national sont intégralement compensées.

b) *Mesures d'effet équivalant à des restrictions quantitatives*

L'arrêt *Dassonville* donne de la « mesure d'effet équivalant à une restriction quantitative » une définition très large : « Toute réglementation commerciale des Etats membres susceptible d'entraver directement ou indirectement, actuellement ou potentiellement, le commerce intracommunautaire » ([17]).

Cette notion peut englober même des mesures qui ne font formellement aucune distinction entre produits nationaux et produits importés, du moment qu'elles entravent, en fait, les importations, tels par exemple des prix maxima (arrêts *SADAM*) ([18]) et *Tasca* ([19]), minima (arrêt *Van Tiggele*) ([20]), fixes (arrêt *GB-INNO-BM*) ([21]), blocages (arrêt *Danis*) ([22]) ou la fixation d'une teneur minimale en alcool (arrêt *Rewe*) ([23]).

Enfin, l'interdiction de l'article 30 a fait l'objet d'une application en matière d'exercice de droits de propriété industrielle, entraînant une limitation sensible des prérogatives reconnues par les droits nationaux aux titulaires des droits de propriété industrielle (arrêts *Deutsche Grammophon* ([24]), *Sterling Drug* ([25]) et *Hag* ([26])).

c) *Règles de concurrence*

L'arrêt *Continental Can* ([27]) a admis l'applicabilité de l'article 86 à une opération de concentration réalisée par une entreprise en position dominan-

---

([17]) Arrêt du 11 juillet 1974, aff. n° 8-74, *Rec.*, 1974, p. 837, 852.
([18]) Arrêt du 26 février 1976, aff. jtes n°s 88 à 90-75, *Rec.*, 1976, p. 323.
([19]) Arrêt du 26 février 1976, aff. n° 65-75, *Rec.*, 1976, p. 291.
([20]) Arrêt du 24 janvier 1978, aff. n° 82-77, *Rec.*, 1978, p. 25.
([21]) Arrêt du 16 novembre 1977, aff. n° 13-77, *Rec.*, 1977, p. 2115.
([22]) Arrêt du 6 novembre 1979, aff. jtes n°s 16 à 20-79, *Rec.*, 1979, p. 3327.
([23]) Arrêt du 20 février 1979, aff. n° 120-78, *Rec.*, 1979, p. 649.
([24]) Arrêt du 8 juin 1971, aff. n° 78-80, *Rec.*, 1971, p. 487.
([25]) Arrêt du 31 octobre 1974, aff. n° 15-74, *Rec.*, 1974, p. 1147.
([26]) Arrêt du 3 juillet 1974, aff. n° 192-73, *Rec.*, 1974, p. 731.
([27]) Arrêt du 21 février 1973, aff. n° 6-72, *Rec.*, 1973, p. 215.

te et dont l'effet était de renforcer cette position au point que le degré de domination atteint entravait substantiellement la concurrence.

Les arrêts *Roubaix-Roux* ([28]) et *De Norre-Concordia* ([29]) ont considéré que, nonobstant le texte clair de l'article 1, paragraphe 2, du règlement n° 67/67, l'exemption par catégorie s'applique aux accords de distribution ou d'approvisionnement exclusifs entre entreprises d'un seul et même Etat membre.

Conclusion

Dans l'ensemble, quoique l'interprétation donnée par la Cour aille sans doute plus loin que ce qui avait été envisagé par les auteurs du traité, il ne semble pas qu'on puisse lui en faire grief. En effet, d'une part, il s'agissait de parer à des entraves « sournoises » dont le nombre et l'ampleur n'avaient pas été clairement perçus à l'époque où les traités furent négociés, les entraves directes telles que droits de douane, contingentements, ... accaparant l'attention en raison de leur caractère beaucoup plus visible. Il s'agissait, d'autre part, de faire face à des phénomènes nouveaux qui appelaient une solution au niveau communautaire, tels que le développement considérable du phénomène de concentration économique, ou le recours systématique aux droits de propriété industrielle pour cloisonner les marchés.

Certaines réserves peuvent toutefois être émises : ainsi l'arrêt *Hag* paraît être allé plus loin que ne l'exigeaient les circonstances, dans la mesure où il impose le principe de la libre circulation des produits portant des marques ayant une origine commune, même lorsque le fractionnement de la marque résulte d'une mesure de contrainte publique antérieure à l'entrée en vigueur du traité.

De même, dans les arrêts *Roubaix-Roux* et *De Norre-Concordia,* l'interprétation *contra legem* s'imposait d'autant moins que le règlement en cause émanait de la Commission, laquelle est moins sujette à des « blocages » d'origine politique que le Conseil. Il nous semble que la Cour devrait faire preuve d'une plus grande prudence dans son recours à l'interprétation téléologique lorsque la matière dans laquelle elle est appelée à intervenir est susceptible de faire l'objet d'une réglementation efficace par la Communauté.

C. LA NAISSANCE D'UN ORDRE JURIDIQUE NOUVEAU

En affirmant que « la Communauté constitue un nouvel ordre juridique de droit international, au profit duquel les Etats ont limité, bien que

([28]) Arrêt du 3 février 1976, aff. n° 63-75, *Rec.*, 1976, p. 111.
([29]) Arrêt du 1er février 1977, aff. n° 47-76, *Rec.*, 1977, p. 65.

dans des domaines restreints, leurs droits souverains, et dont les sujets sont non seulement les Etats membres mais également leurs ressortissants » (arrêts *Van Gend en Loos* (30) et *Costa* (31)), la Cour de justice a jeté les prémisses indispensables aux théories de l'*applicabilité directe* et de la *primauté* du droit communautaire qui, sans aucun doute, constituent les piliers irréductibles de ce droit.

L'attribution d'un *effet direct,* à certaines conditions, à la norme communautaire engendre « le droit pour toute personne de demander à son juge de lui appliquer traités, règlements, directives ou décisions communautaires » et entraîne parallèlement « l'obligation pour le juge de faire usage de ces textes quelle que soit la législation du pays dont il relève » (32).

L'applicabilité directe a eu pour principal effet de faire du droit communautaire une réalité concrète et vivante, fournissant au citoyen européen, dont l'identité juridique s'est ainsi progressivement précisée, un ensemble de prérogatives pouvant être directement invoquées devant le juge de l'ordre interne tant à l'encontre de l'autorité publique (effet vertical) que dans les rapports avec d'autres particuliers (effet horizontal ; voy. les arrêts *Bosch* (33), *Walrave* (34) et *Defrenne* II (35)).

De la sorte, le justiciable européen a été incité, d'une part, à demander de plus en plus fréquemment à son juge national de constater et de sanctionner l'incompabilité entre une norme interne et une norme communautaire directement applicable ou estimée telle et, d'autre part, à dénoncer à la Commission les inobservations de nature législative, exécutive ou administrative du droit communautaire, de manière à permettre à cette dernière d'exercer les compétences et les responsabilités qui sont les siennes dans l'accomplissement de la procédure en constatation de manquement des Etats membres.

Il s'ensuit que le contrôle de l'exécution par les Etats membres de leurs obligations communautaires s'est trouvé considérablement renforcé dans la pratique : multiplication des recours préjudiciels en interprétation qui est le corollaire de l'accroissement des litiges portés par les particuliers devant le juge de l'ordre interne ; multiplication des procédures en constatation de manquement. Ces circonstances peuvent expliquer la naissance d'un sentiment de frustration de la part des autorités publiques nationales qui font l'objet d'assignations accrues tant au plan national qu'au plan communautaire, d'autant plus que la procédure écrite applicable au régime des ques-

---

(30) Arrêt du 5 février 1963, aff. nº 26-62, *Rec.*, vol. IX, p. 1.
(31) Arrêt du 15 juillet 1964, aff. nº 6-64, *Rec.*, vol. X, p. 1141.
(32) R. LECOURT, *L'Europe des juges*, Bruxelles 1976, p. 248.
(33) Arrêt du 6 avril 1962, aff. nº 13-61, *Rec.*, vol. VIII, p. 89.
(34) Arrêt du 12 décembre 1974, aff. nº 36-74, *Rec.*, 1974, p. 1405.
(35) Arrêt du 8 avril 1976, aff. nº 43-75, *Rec.*, 1976, p. 455.

tions préjudicielles ne prévoit que la présentation d'un seul mémoire, à la différence de la procédure écrite régissant les autres contentieux portés à la connaissance de la Cour de justice.

Cela dit, si la théorie de l'effet direct comme la procédure en constatation de manquement poursuivent, par des voies différentes, le même objectif, à savoir le respect du droit communautaire par les autorités publiques, certaines questions restent ouvertes.

Ainsi, les effets de la théorie de l'applicabilité directe se heurtent à la règle de l'autonomie de la procédure en vertu de laquelle les juridictions nationales chargées d'assurer la protection juridique découlant pour les justiciables de l'effet direct, ne peuvent le faire qu'en appliquant les règles du droit procédural interne (arrêts *Rewe-Zentralfinanz* (36) et *Comet* (37)). Or, ces règles sont différentes d'Etat à Etat (notamment en ce qui concerne la désignation de la juridiction compétente, les délais de recours, l'organisation même des recours, le régime des sanctions nationales applicables...). Il ne pourra être remédié à cette situation, qui constitue une limite aux effets internes de l'applicabilité directe, que par une action de coordination communautaire et un rapprochement spontané ou conventionnel des législations nationales.

D'autre part, s'il est vrai qu'un arrêt de la Cour constatant le manquement d'un Etat membre à une disposition de droit communautaire directement applicable, peut être invoqué devant le juge interne à l'appui d'une action visant à faire écarter l'application de la loi nationale, on peut se demander s'il en est de même au cas où la Cour sanctionne un manquement à une disposition de droit communautaire non directement applicable.

Quant à la *primauté* reconnue au droit communautaire sur le droit interne, elle a eu surtout pour effet de renforcer considérablement l'efficacité du droit communautaire. La Cour, dès l'affaire *Costa* (38), a clairement et irrévocablement établi qu'en raison de la nature juridique spécifique de la Communauté, les Etats membres se trouvaient désormais dans l'impossibilité « de faire prévaloir, contre un ordre juridique accepté par eux sur une base de réciprocité, une mesure unilatérale ultérieure qui ne saurait ainsi lui être opposable ».

La règle de la primauté est absolue. Elle ne tolère aucune exception sous peine de provoquer la dislocation de la notion de Communauté. Une norme de droit communautaire directement applicable, qu'elle soit contenue dans une disposition du traité constitutif ou dans un acte de droit dérivé, ne peut donc se voir valablement opposer un acte de droit interne, quelle

(36) Arrêt du 16 décembre 1976, aff. nº 33-76, *Rec.*, 1976, p. 1989.
(37) Arrêt du 16 décembre 1976, aff. nº 45-76, *Rec.*, 1976, p. 2043.
(38) *Loc. cit.*

que soit la place de cet acte dans la hiérarchie des normes nationales et quelle que soit la date à laquelle cet acte est entré en vigueur.

L'effet combiné de la primauté et de l'applicabilité directe a pour conséquence « non seulement de rendre inapplicable de plein droit (...) toute disposition contraire de la législation nationale existante, mais encore (...) d'empêcher la formation valable de nouveaux actes législatifs nationaux dans la mesure où ils seraient incompatibles avec des normes communautaires » (affaire *Simmenthal*) ([39]). Ce dernier membre de phrase a été interprété par un commentateur comme consacrant la théorie selon laquelle « les Etats membres ne sont plus juridiquement en droit d'adopter des mesures empiétant sur le domaine réservé à la Communauté ou autrement incompatibles avec les dispositions du droit communautaire », en sorte que le problème général du conflit entre droit communautaire et droit national serait réglé dans le sens qu'il ne saurait juridiquement exister ([40]).

II. LA DOCTRINE DE LA COUR ET L'EVOLUTION DE LA COMMUNAUTE

A. LA JURISPRUDENCE COMMUNAUTAIRE ET LES JURIDICTIONS NATIONALES

La réflexion sur l'influence de la doctrine de la Cour et l'évolution de la Communauté doit comporter une brève évocation de l'attitude des juridictions nationales en ce qui concerne le droit communautaire.

En effet, la jurisprudence peut incontestablement être un facteur d'intégration et les juridictions nationales sont des organes des Etats membres, comme l'a opportunément rappelé la Cour de justice dans son arrêt *Simmenthal* ([41]). Cela signifie, entre autres, qu'elles peuvent être les sujets de manquement d'Etat, soumis à la procédure de constatation des infractions prévue par les traités ([42]). On ne peut dès lors négliger l'attitude des juridictions nationales dans une appréciation du comportement des Etats membres.

---

(39) Arrêt du 9 mars 1978, aff. n° 106-77, *Rec.*, 1978, p. 629.

(40) A. Barav, Les effets du droit communautaire directement applicable, *Cah. dr. eur.*, 1978, p. 260 et suiv.

(41) Cité *supra*, note (39). Cela ne signifie pas que, lorsqu'elles appliquent le droit communautaire, les juridictions ne sont pas aussi des juridictions communautaires. Voy. D. Carreau, Droit communautaire et droits nationaux: concurrence ou primauté? *Rev. trim. dr. eur.*, 1978, p. 381 et suiv., spéc. p. 417-418.

(42) On sait que la doctrine a parfois émis des réserves à ce sujet. Voy. J. Mertens de Wilmars et Y. Verougstraete, Proceedings against Member States for Failure to Fulfil Obligations? *CML Rev.*, 1970, p. 385 et suiv..
Il est évident que de simples erreurs de droit ou de fait ne constituent pas des manquements. Il faut qu'il s'agisse de violations caractérisées du droit communautaire, telles que la méconnaissance systématique des obligations découlant de l'article 177 ou des compétences de la Cour.

Les juridictions ont généralement témoigné d'une grande réceptivité à l'égard de la doctrine de la Cour, qu'il s'agisse des principes fondamentaux de l'ordre juridique communautaire (effet direct, primauté) ou de l'interprétation du droit matériel.

En ce qui concerne la primauté, on doit relever des évolutions saisissantes, voire des retournements spectaculaires de la jurisprudence dans certains Etats membres (43). De tels développements eussent été impensables sans la jurisprudence de la Cour de justice. L'importance donnée à l'effet direct par celle-ci a ouvert un vaste champ d'action aux juridictions nationales en faisant du droit communautaire une réalité qui se manifeste au niveau même des particuliers et non pas seulement à celui des Etats et des institutions.

Les résistances qui restent isolées en ont été d'autant plus spectaculaires.

On sait que la Cour constitutionnelle allemande, par son ordonnance du 29 mai 1974 (44), a prétendu exercer son contrôle sur le respect par les institutions communautaires, dans l'exercice de leur pouvoir réglementaire, des droits fondamentaux consacrés par la Loi fondamentale de la République fédérale. Une décision récente laisse espérer toutefois une évolution. La Cour constitutionnelle a laissé ouverte, dans une ordonnance du 25 juillet 1979, la question de savoir si elle maintient la jurisprudence de sa *Solange-Beschluss* (45). Peut-être aura-t-elle l'occasion dans un avenir proche de modifier sa doctrine ?

L'attitude du Conseil d'Etat de France est aussi préoccupante. L'arrêt que la haute juridiction a rendu en assemblée plénière, le 20 novembre 1978, a révélé de façon éclatante les abus de la théorie de l'acte clair utilisée par le Conseil d'Etat pour refuser d'avoir recours au mécanisme préjudiciel (46).

(43) Cette évolution a été souvent décrite. Nous nous permettons de renvoyer à W.J. GANSHOF VAN DER MEERSCH, L'ordre juridique des Communautés européennes et le droit international, extrait du *RCADI*, vol. V., 1975, Alphen aan den Rijn, 1978, p. 213 à 231; Ph. COUVREUR, L'adhésion de l'Espagne aux Communautés européennes: l'ordre juridique communautaire, in *L'Espagne et les Communautés européennes. Problèmes posés par l'adhésion*, Bruxelles, 1979, p. 135 et suiv., spéc. p. 144 et suiv. ainsi que les auteurs cités; G. BEBR, How Supreme is Community Law in the National Courts?, *CML Rev.*, 1974, p. 3 à 37; du même auteur, A Critical Review of Recent Cases Law of National Courts, *CML Rev.*, 1974, p. 408-431.

(44) *BVerf. GE* 37, 271 et suiv.; texte français avec note de G. COHEN-JONATHAN, *Cah. dr. eur.*, 1975, p. 149 et suiv.

(45) *B Verf* G, 25 juillet 1979, *EuGRZ*, 1979, p. 547.

(46) Dans une affaire récente concernant le régime de l'alcool, qui a donné lieu à l'arrêt du 27 juillet 1979 — où le Conseil d'Etat a utilisé l'argument fondé sur la clarté des dispositions communautaires en cause —, le commissaire du gouvernement a établi des statistiques impressionnantes sur l'attitude du Conseil d'Etat en matière de renvoi préjudiciel. Mises à jour, ces données révèlent que, dans une quinzaine d'affaires, les dispositions ont été jugées claires et le Conseil d'Etat s'est abstenu de saisir la Cour. Il a posé six fois des questions préjudicielles et, dans deux cas, il ne l'a pas fait en se référant expressément à la jurisprudence antérieure de la Cour. Voy. Conseil d'Etat, 27 juillet 1979, Assemblée, *Syndicat national des fabricants de spiritueux consommés à l'eau*, AJDA, 20 novembre 1979, p. 36 et suiv., spéc. p. 41-42.

En l'occurrence, le Conseil d'Etat a considéré comme claires les dispositions de l'article 189, en leur donnant une interprétation contraire à celle de la Cour de justice. On peut difficilement imaginer violation plus manifeste de l'obligation de saisine imposée aux juridictions statuant en dernière instance par l'article 177, alinéa 2 et de l'autorité due aux arrêts de la Cour rendus en matière préjudicielle ([47]).

Si l'on peut comprendre — sans nécessairement approuver — les scrupules du juge qui est le gardien de la constitutionnalité interne, en revanche, l'attitude du Conseil d'Etat apparaît comme un acte de rébellion d'autant plus injustifié qu'il était, dans les circonstances de l'espèce, gratuit. On voit qu'ici le débat n'est plus entre les mérites ou les inconvénients de la théorie de l'acte clair. Il est entre le refus ou l'acceptation des implications de l'intégration sur le plan judiciaire.

Près d'un an plus tard, le Conseil d'Etat devait témoigner du même esprit dans des arrêts qui, pour avoir été moins remarqués, n'en sont pas moins importants et regrettables. Il a, statuant dans le cadre du contentieux ouvert à propos de l'élection du Parlement européen, confirmé la doctrine qu'il avait adoptée en 1968 en refusant la primauté au traité et au droit communautaire. Pour le Conseil d'Etat, malgré l'attitude adoptée par la Cour de cassation, reconnaître la valeur supérieure d'un traité par rapport à une loi, c'est toujours contrôler la constitutionnalité de cette loi ([48]).

B. L'INFLUENCE DE LA JURISPRUDENCE DE LA COUR SUR LA PRATIQUE DES ETATS MEMBRES ET DES INSTITUTIONS

La Cour de justice a eu un rôle moteur dans certains domaines. Dans d'autres, sa jurisprudence n'a pas réussi à surmonter des blocages incontestables. Dans certains cas, on peut même se demander si elle n'a pas contribué à les consolider.

([47]) On sait que le Conseil d'Etat a refusé au particulier le droit d'invoquer une disposition d'une directive à l'encontre d'un acte administratif individuel. En revanche, et assez paradoxalement, la haute juridiction admet le droit pour le particulier d'invoquer l'irrégularité, par rapport à une directive, des dispositions réglementaires d'application.
La littérature sur l'arrêt *Cohn-Bendit* est déjà vaste et en sens divers, quoique généralement critique. Voy. J. Boulouis, L'applicabilité directe des directives. A propos d'un arrêt Cohn-Bendit du Conseil d'Etat, *RMC*, 1979, p. 104; G. Isaac, Le juge administratif français et les directives communautaires, *Cah. dr. eur.*, 1979, p. 265 et suiv.; *D.*, 1979, p. 155 avec note B. Pacteau; *Rev. trim. dr. comm.*, 1979, avec note, A. Lyon-Caen, p. 647; *JCP*, 1979, II, 1958, avec note R. Kovar; *Clunet*, 1979, note B. Goldmann, p. 591, etc...

([48]) Voy. Conseil d'Etat, 22 octobre 1979 *AJDA*, 1980, p. 39 avec note B.G.

La carence des Etats membres et des institutions a incité la Cour de justice à jouer un rôle de législateur. Sa jurisprudence dynamique amène à se demander jusqu'à quel point il lui est possible de prendre le risque de ne pas être suivie.

1) Dans des cas nombreux et souvent techniques, la Cour a eu une influence sur l'action du législateur.

Ainsi, le règlement n° 1408/71 concernant la sécurité sociale des travailleurs qui se déplacent dans la Communauté et de leurs familles est-il en grande partie la codification de la jurisprudence de la Cour dans l'interprétation des règlements nos 3 et 4 concernant la sécurité sociale des travailleurs migrants.

Le règlement n° 2988/74 relatif à la prescription en matière de poursuites et d'exécution dans les domaines du droit des transports et de la concurrence de la CEE est la suite directe de la constatation par la Cour d'une lacune de la réglementation communautaire de la concurrence dans les arrêts du 15 juillet 1970 relatifs à l'entente de la quinine.

Le règlement n° 1681/79 en matière de dumping est en partie le résultat de la jurisprudence de la Cour dans les affaires de roulements à bille japonais et des observations critiques formulées par l'avocat général Warner dans ses conclusions à l'égard de la pratique suivie par la Commission dans l'application du règlement n° 459/68.

Il s'agissait notamment du problème de la légitimité de la perception de droits provisoires en cas d'acceptation par les autorités communautaires d'engagements de revision de prix et de la communication de renseignements par la Commission aux firmes en cause.

Dans tous ces cas, il n'a jamais été contesté que la Cour est restée dans son rôle.

On pourrait multiplier les exemples.

2) Dans certains domaines, la Cour a débloqué une situation qui s'enlisait en raison de la carence du Conseil. Elle a pu le faire en se fondant sur l'article 8, paragraphe 7 du traité selon lequel la période de transition constitue le terme extrême pour l'entrée en vigueur de l'ensemble des règles prévues et pour la mise en place de l'ensemble des réalisations que comporte l'établissement du marché commun.

Ainsi, l'arrêt *Reyners* ([49]) a reconnu l'effet direct à l'interdiction de discrimination selon la nationalité pour l'exercice de la profession d'avocat,

---

([49]) Aff. n° 2-74, arrêt du 21 juin 1974, *Rec.*, 1974, p. 631 et suiv.

et cela en l'absence des directives du Conseil qui devaient mettre en œuvre la liberté d'établissement.

Cet arrêt, suivi de plusieurs autres en matière de liberté d'établissement et de libre prestation des services, a permis à la Commission de retirer des propositions de directives dont l'objet était de conférer le droit d'établissement, pour concentrer ses efforts ainsi que ceux du Conseil sur la préparation de directives de coordination destinées à faciliter l'exercice des activités non salariées. Des progrès ont ainsi pu être accomplis en ce qui concerne les professions libérales, des activités d'assurance et des activités bancaires.

De même, la reconnaissance de l'effet direct de l'article 37, dans l'arrêt *Manghera* ([50]), a permis de réaliser l'aménagement des monopoles d'Etat à caractère commercial de façon à en éliminer les principaux caractères restrictifs des échanges.

3) En revanche, l'affirmation de l'application de plein droit des règles générales sur la libre circulation des marchandises dès la fin de la période de transition aux produits non couverts par une organisation de marché n'a pas eu l'effet d'accélérer l'action du législateur en ce qui concerne l'adoption d'une politique commune pour les bananes (arrêt *Charmasson*) ([51]) et les pommes de terre (arrêts *Meijer c. Department of Trade* et *Commission c. Royaume-Uni*) ([52]). Peut-être, pour la viande ovine (arrêt *Commission c. France*) ([53]) en ira-t-il autrement en raison même de l'importance politique du dossier.

De même, la proposition de règlement sur le contrôle des concentrations préparée par la Commission dans le sillage de l'arrêt *Continental Can* ([54]) a fait l'objet sur le plan politique d'importantes réserves de plusieurs Etats membres et ne semble pas près d'être adoptée.

On pourrait se demander si le succès ou l'insuccès de la Cour en l'occurrence ne sont pas fonction des intérêts concernés et, lorsqu'il s'agit d'une question très politique, de la dramatisation du dossier au niveau législatif, plutôt que de la force de persuasion de la doctrine de la Cour. Mais ce n'est pas un motif suffisant pour critiquer la haute juridiction. Il est en effet incontestable qu'en considérant que les règles sur la libre circulation des marchandises doivent s'appliquer intégralement dans tous les domaines dès la fin de la période de transition, y compris aux produits agricoles ne faisant pas

---

([50]) Aff. n° 59-75, arrêt du 3 février 1976, *Rec.*, 1976, p. 91 et suiv.

([51]) Aff. n° 48-74, arrêt du 2 décembre 1974, *Rec.*, 1974, p. 1383 et suiv.

([52]) Aff. n° 118-78, arrêt du 29 mars 1979, *Rec.*, 1979, p. 1387 et suiv. et aff. n° 231-78, arrêt du 29 mars 1979, *Rec.*, 1979, p. 44 et suiv.

([53]) Aff. n° 232-78, arrêt du 25 septembre 1979, *Rec.*, 1979, p. 2729.

([54]) Aff. n° 6-72, arrêt du 21 février 1973, *Rec.*, 1973, p. 215 et suiv.

l'objet d'une organisation commune de marché, la Cour s'est comportée strictement comme un organe juridictionnel. Elle a appliqué les règles qui lui paraissaient se dégager du traité. Lui reprocher de n'avoir pas tenu compte de la situation créée par la carence du Conseil revient à lui reprocher de n'avoir pas eu égard à un élément extra-juridique. La Cour ne peut, en effet, infléchir la portée de la règle en fonction de l'importance politique plus ou moins grande d'une question ou d'un changement prétendu de la volonté des auteurs du traité qui ne se serait pas exprimée par les voies que celui-ci ouvre pour sa revision.

C. LA COUR ET LES REALITES POLITIQUES

1) Le droit des relations extérieures

On connaît les grandes étapes de la jurisprudence en ce qui concerne les relations extérieures : arrêt *AETR* ([55]), avis n° 1-75 ([56]), arrêt *Kramer* ([57]), avis n° 1-76 ([58]), délibération n° 1-78 ([59]) et avis n° 1-78 ([60]).

Les enseignements de cette jurisprudence sont essentiellement :

— la reconnaissance de la compétence implicite de conclure des accords,

— l'affirmation de la compétence exclusive en matière de politique commerciale et dans les domaines où existent des règles communes sur le plan interne.

Dans ces deux directions, la position des Etats membres ou de certains d'entre eux était soit franchement hostile, soit réservée sinon en droit, au moins dans les faits.

On peut s'interroger sur l'effet de la doctrine de la Cour sur la pratique des institutions.

A cet égard, il est indéniable qu'il faut attribuer à la doctrine de l'arrêt *AETR* la conclusion par la Communauté de nombreux accords — notamment multilatéraux — dans des hypothèses où sa participation apparaissait comme impossible auparavant.

([55]) Aff. n° 22-70, arrêt du 31 mars 1971, *Rec.*, 1971, p. 263 et suiv.

([56]) Avis du 11 novembre 1975, *Rec.*, 1975, p. 1355 et suiv.

([57]) Aff. jtes n°s 3, 4 et 6-76, *Kramer e.a.*, *Rec.*, 1976, p. 1279 et suiv.

([58]) Avis du 26 avril 1977, *Rec.*, 1977, p. 741 et suiv.

([59]) Délibération du 14 novembre 1978, *Rec.* 1978, p. 2151 et suiv.

([60]) *JOCE*, n° C 279, 8 novembre 1979.

Tous les accords en matière de pêche reposent sur la jurisprudence de l'arrêt *Kramer* et de l'avis n° 1-76.

La conclusion par la Communauté seule de la quasi-totalité des accords issus des négociations commerciales multilatérales (*Tokyo Round*) a été rendue possible par l'avis n° 1-78, alors même que les Etats membres étaient très divisés sur l'étendue de la compétence communautaire à cet égard.

Même la délibération n° 1-78, malgré les controverses qu'elle a suscitées, a eu des suites positives tant en ce qui concerne la participation d'Euratom à des accords internationaux (61) que dans la perspective enfin débloquée d'une revision du chapitre VI en matière d'approvisionnement.

Il est toutefois incontestable qu'en dépit de la jurisprudence, la politique commerciale ne relève pas encore entièrement de la compétence exclusive de la Communauté. Les accords de coopération, notamment avec les pays socialistes, resteront sans doute longtemps encore l'apanage des Etats malgré la doctrine de l'avis n° 1-78, qui consacre une conception large de la politique commerciale.

L'avis n° 1-76 a fait l'objet de réserves aussi vives en raison de ce qui est apparu, de la part de la Cour, comme une incompréhension manifeste des spécificités de l'accord à conclure avec la Suisse en matière de réglementation de la navigation sur le Rhin, matière qui n'intéressait pas tous les Etats membres.

D'où la tentation de reprocher à la Cour son irréalisme et la suggestion que sa jurisprudence vient à l'appui de développements inévitables. La Cour ne pourrait infléchir des volontés politiques résolues. Si elle prétendait le faire, elle échouerait.

A cette critique, on peut opposer les deux niveaux auxquels se situe le raisonnement de la Cour : sur le plan des principes, la majeure qui dégage la règle est impérieuse ; dans l'application de cette règle à des cas concrets, la Cour admet des solutions pragmatiques, ménageant les intérêts des Etats.

Ainsi, a-t-elle justifié la « délégation » par la Communauté à ses Etats membres du pouvoir de conclure l'AETR, au risque d'ouvrir la porte au recours à ce procédé dans des conditions contestables. Elle affirme le caractère exclusif de la compétence en matière de politique commerciale commune mais elle souligne, d'une part, le caractère progressif de son élaboration

(61) On songe à la participation d'Euratom à l'accord d'approvisionnement à conclure avec l'Australie et aux négociations qui ont fait l'objet de la demande d'avis du gouvernement belge en vertu de l'article 103 du traité instituant la CECA et qui portent sur la sécurité « physique » des matières fissiles.

(avis n° 1-75) et, d'autre part, le droit de participation des Etats à la conclusion de l'accord dès lors que l'on se trouve sur un terrain qui relève de leur compétence réservée (avis n° 1-78).

Elle admet la légitimité de la conclusion mixte de l'accord d'immobilisation de la navigation du Rhin dans l'avis n° 1-76, dans la mesure où la participation des Etats concrétise leur engagement de modifier les conventions de Mannheim et de la Moselle avec lesquelles l'accord projeté est incompatible.

2) La libre circulation des marchandises

Ici aussi, l'affirmation très ferme du principe fondamental de la liberté des échanges s'est accompagnée d'une reconnaissance des nécessités pratiques auxquelles les Etats membres peuvent parfois être confrontés.

Ainsi, la jurisprudence relative à l'application de l'article 30 aux réglementations nationales de prix s'accompagne du rappel que les organisations communes de marché mettent à la disposition des Etats membres les moyens de parer aux difficultés conjoncturelles qui pourraient survenir.

De même, l'arrêt *Bauhuis* (62) admet la légalité de la perception d'une redevance par les Etats membres lorsqu'ils accomplissent des opérations de contrôle de salubrité en exécution des directives de rapprochement des législations vétérinaires et sanitaires.

De même, l'arrêt *Rewe* de 1979 (63) considère que les obstacles à la circulation intracommunautaire résultant de disparités des législations nationales doivent être acceptés dans la mesure où ces prescriptions sont nécessaires pour satisfaire à des exigences impératives tenant, notamment, à l'efficacité des contrôles fiscaux, à la protection de la santé publique, à la loyauté des transactions commerciales et à la défense des consommateurs.

3) La politique agricole commune

La mise en œuvre de la politique agricole commune pose le délicat problème de la répartition des compétences entre les institutions communautaires et les Etats membres.

La diversité des problèmes et des solutions impose une approche pragmatique fondée sur l'existence ou non d'organisations communes de marché.

---

(62) Arrêt du 25 janvier 1977, aff. n° 46-76, *Rec.*, 1977, p. 5.

(63) Précité.

a) *En cas d'existence d'organisation commune de marché*

Dans l'hypothèse d'une organisation commune de marché instituée conformément à l'article 40 du traité CEE, les Etats membres sont tenus de s'abstenir de toute mesure qui serait de nature à y déroger et à y porter atteinte (arrêt *Amsterdam Bulb*) ([64]).

En particulier, lorsque l'organisation commune comporte un régime communautaire de prix, « les Etats membres ne peuvent plus intervenir, par des dispositions nationales prises unilatéralement, dans le mécanisme de la formation des prix tel qu'il résulte de l'organisation commune » (arrêt *Galli*) ([65]). Il s'ensuit que, si la fixation des prix communs concerne le stade de la production et du commerce de gros, les Etats membres conservent en principe « — sans préjudice d'autres dispositions du traité — le pouvoir de prendre les mesures appropriées en matière de formation des prix aux stades du commerce de détail et de la consommation, à condition qu'elles ne mettent pas en danger les objectifs ou le fonctionnement de l'organisation commune du marché en question » (même arrêt). Il y a toutefois lieu de penser que, si les Etats conservent intact ce pouvoir, une réglementation nationale des prix au stade de la vente au consommateur final ne manquera pas, dans certaines circonstances, de se répercuter sur la formation communautaire des prix aux stades antérieurs. On pouvait donc s'attendre à ce que la Cour de justice interdise toute intervention des Etats dans le régime de fixation des prix, à quelque stade que ce soit, dès lors qu'il pouvait en résulter une affectation directe ou indirecte sur le système de fixation des prix communs.

Or, à cet égard, il y a lieu de constater que, bien au contraire, la Cour a, en quelque sorte, « restitué » aux Etats membres leur pouvoir d'intervenir par des dispositions nationales prises unilatéralement dans le mécanisme de formation des prix communs, en énonçant « que, en fait, une réglementation nationale en matière de prix agricoles, visant les mêmes stades commerciaux que le régime de prix communautaires, risquera normalement d'entrer en collision avec ledit régime davantage qu'une réglementation s'appliquant exclusivement à d'autres stades » (arrêts *SADAM* ([66]) et *Tasca* ([67])).

Il semble donc qu'on puisse parler, à propos de l'attitude de la Cour d'un certain « pragmatisme » consistant à laisser aux Etats membres l'exercice de compétences dans des domaines qui n'affectent pas directement la réglementation commune.

([64]) Arrêt du 2 février 1977, aff. 50-76, *Rec.*, 1977, p. 137.

([65]) Arrêt du 23 janvier 1975, aff. 31-74, *Rec.*, 1975, p. 47.

([66]) Arrêt du 26 février 1976, aff. jtes n°s 88 à 90-75, *Rec.*, 1976, p. 323.

([67]) Arrêt du 26 février 1976, aff. n° 65-75, *Rec.*, 1976, p. 291.

Pour le reste, l'intervention normative des Etats membres se module cas par cas, en fonction des caractéristiques du droit communautaire.

D'une manière générale, les Etats ne peuvent intervenir qu'en raison d'une habilitation des institutions communautaires pour le compte de la Communauté (arrêt *Roquette*) (68) ou qu'en cas d'existence de mesures d'intervention dans le cadre d'une organisation commune de marché (arrêt *Cucchi*) (69).

Dans le silence des dispositions réglementaires, les Etats sont en droit de prendre les mesures nationales qui ne dérogent pas au régime communautaire, qui n'en limitent pas la portée et qui tendent, au contraire, à la même finalité (arrêts *Amsterdam Bulb* (70), *Van der Hulst* (71), *Van den Hazel* (72) et *Pigs Marketing Board* (73)).

Le pouvoir d'intervention des Etats membres en vue de combler les lacunes des règlements communautaires et de pourvoir aux mesures d'exécution nationales nécessaires, doit donc se faire sur la base d'une interprétation à la fois téléologique et fonctionnaliste.

b) *En l'absence d'organisation commune de marché*

Dans l'affaire *Charmasson* (74), la Cour de justice a admis qu'une organisation nationale de marché pouvait, pendant la période transitoire, déroger aux règles générales du traité pour autant que ces dérogations s'avèrent nécessaires pour assurer le fonctionnement de l'organisation nationale sans toutefois entraver les adaptations que comporte l'établissement de la politique agricole commune.

A l'expiration de la période de transition, il n'appartient plus aux Etats membres de déroger aux règles générales du traité qui doivent désormais trouver une application intégrale, et en particulier les règles relatives à la libre circulation des marchandises.

Cette doctrine a été réaffirmée dans l'affaire *Commission c. France* (75) où la Cour a notamment relevé que l'absence d'organisation commune de marchés pour certains produits agricoles (comme la pomme de terre) n'équi-

(68) Arrêt du 21 mai 1976, aff. n° 26-74, *Rec.*, 1976, p. 686.

(69) Arrêt du 25 mai 1977, aff. n° 77-76, *Rec.*, 1977, p. 987.

(70) *Loc. cit.*

(71) Arrêt du 23 janvier 1975, aff. n° 51-74, *Rec.*, 1975, p. 79.

(72) Arrêt du 18 mai 1977, aff. n° 111-76, *Rec.*, 1977, p. 901.

(73) Arrêt du 29 novembre 1978, aff. n° 83-78, *Rec.*, 1978, p. 2347.

(74) Arrêt du 10 décembre 1974, aff. n° 48-74, *Rec.*, 1974, p. 1383.

(75) Arrêt du 16 mars 1977, aff. n° 68-76, *Rec.*, 1977, p. 515.

vaut pas pour autant à un vide juridique que les Etats seraient en droit de combler. Les articles 39 à 46 du traité restent, en effet, applicables. Or, dans la mesure où l'article 38, paragraphe 1, dispose que le marché commun s'étend à l'agriculture et que le paragraphe 2 de ce même article renforce ce principe, les dispositions de l'article 34 interdisant les restrictions quantitatives et les mesures d'effet équivalent à l'exportation sont applicables. Les dispositions des articles 39 à 46 ne sauraient être invoquées pour justifier une dérogation unilatérale aux exigences de l'article 34 du traité.

L'expiration de la période de transition entraîne donc à la fois l'application intégrale des règles du traité aux produits agricoles non encore soumis à une organisation commune de marché et le dessaisissement des Etats membres dont les compétences sont désormais exclusivement exercées par les institutions communautaires auxquelles il appartient d'arrêter les mesures susceptibles de constituer, dans le cadre communautaire, une solution conforme à l'intérêt général de la Communauté.

Les mêmes principes s'appliquent dans les relations entre les Etats membres originaires et les trois nouveaux Etats membres au fur et à mesure que ceux-ci sont astreints au respect des dispositions du traité en fonction de l'échéancier contenu dans l'acte d'adhésion.

A cet égard, la question s'est posée dans l'affaire 231/78 (*Commission c. Royaume-Uni de Grande-Bretagne et d'Irlande du Nord* ([76]) de savoir si l'article 60, paragraphe 2 de l'acte d'adhésion qui prévoit pour les produits non soumis, lors de l'adhésion, à une organisation commune de marché, mais faisant partie d'une organisation nationale de marché, la non application des règles relatives à la suppression des taxes d'effet équivalant à des droits de douane et des restrictions quantitatives et mesures d'effet équivalent jusqu'à l'entrée en vigueur d'une organisation commune, constitue une « disposition particulière » au sens de l'article 9, paragraphe 2 du même acte selon lequel: « Sous réserve des dates, délais et dispositions particuliers prévus par le présent acte, l'application des mesures transitoires s'achève à la fin de l'année 1977 ».

Dans ses conclusions, fort bien argumentées, l'avocat général Mayras a estimé que la persistance de restrictions quantitatives, au-delà du 1er janvier 1978, découlant des dispositions réglementant, au Royaume-Uni, l'organisation nationale de la pomme de terre, n'était pas contraire à l'article 60, paragraphe 2 de l'acte d'adhésion « pour autant que ces mesures fissent partie d'une organisation nationale de marché en vigueur à la date de l'adhé-

---

([76]) Arrêt du 29 mars 1979 (Pommes de terre), *Rec.*, 1979, p. 1447.
Voy. aussi l'arrêt du même jour, aff. n° 118/78, *Meijer*, *Rec.*, 1979, p. 1387.

sion et dans la mesure nécessaire pour assurer le maintien de l'organisation nationale en attendant la réalisation de l'organisation commune de marché » ([77]).

La Cour n'a pas suivi son avocat général. Elle a préféré s'en tenir strictement, en dépit des textes, au schéma jurisprudentiel inauguré par l'arrêt *Charmasson*. Sans doute la Cour a-t-elle été principalement animée du souci de n'introduire aucune différence de traitement entre le régime applicable aux Etats membres originaires et celui valant pour les nouveaux Etats membres. Il n'empêche que, même si cette motivation est parfaitement compréhensible, il est difficile de suivre la Cour lorsque celle-ci, pour justifier sa position en droit, en vient à interpréter l'article 9, paragraphe 2 de l'acte d'adhésion comme visant par l'expression « dispositions particulières » uniquement celles « d'une nature bien circonscrite et déterminée dans le temps, mais non une disposition qui se réfère à un événement futur et incertain, telle que le paragraphe 2 de l'article 60 » ([78]).

La Cour ne fait-elle pas là le saut qui la fait passer d'un pragmatisme dogmatique à un dogmatisme pragmatique ?

En tout cas, la Cour a réaffirmé sans concession sa jurisprudence dans un arrêt ultérieur se rapportant au régime mis en place par le gouvernement français face aux importations massives de viande ovine en provenance du Royaume-Uni. Ce régime se caractérisait essentiellement par la détermination d'un prix de seuil protégé par un système d'interdiction d'importation et la perception d'une redevance à l'importation en provenance d'un autre Etat membre. Il était indubitablement contraire aux articles 12 et 30 du traité CEE. Le gouvernement français ne contestait d'ailleurs pas ce fait, mais tentait de justifier son attitude en faisant valoir les trois arguments suivants : d'une part, le risque économique qui pourrait résulter du démantèlement de l'organisation nationale du marché en cause ; d'autre part, le danger d'intercaler une phase de libre-échange entre la suppression de l'organisation nationale de marché et le remplacement de celle-ci par une organisation commune, et, enfin, l'attitude du Royaume-Uni qui avait laissé subsister, au mépris du traité, une organisation nationale fondée sur le système des *deficiency payments* dont l'effet est de subventionner des exportations de viande ovine vers la France. En établissant que la France avait violé les articles 12 et 30 du traité CEE depuis le 1er janvier 1978, la Cour n'a guère surpris ceux qui suivent de près l'évolution de sa jurisprudence. On ne peut manquer toutefois d'être, dans les circonstances de l'espèce, frappé par le

---

([77]) *Rec.*, 1979, p. 1419.
([78]) Attendu 16 *in fine*, p. 1462.

caractère rigoureux et absolu avec lequel la Cour rappelle les règles dégagées depuis l'arrêt *Charmasson* et, à l'inverse, par la réfutation rapide que la Cour oppose aux thèses du gouvernement français (79).

On peut espérer que l'affirmation absolue de certains principes par la Cour n'affaiblira pas la crédibilité de ses arrêts. Le risque n'est-il pas grand lorsque, comme dans le cas d'espèce, l'arrêt rendu intervient dans un domaine où les Etats font preuve d'une sensibilité exacerbée et que son exécution dépend en grande partie du bon vouloir des Etats, lui-même fondé sur l'acceptation et le respect mutuels des règles du traité ?

(79) Arrêt du 25 septembre 1979, aff. nº 232-78, *Commission c. République française*, *Rec.*, 1979, p. 2729.

DISCUSSION

M. RYZIGER, *président*

Je remercie les rapporteurs de leurs exposés remarquables. Ces trois exposés se caractérisent par l'optimisme de leurs conclusions et aucun n'a comporté de critiques virulentes à l'égard de l'action de la Cour. L'opposition viendra-t-elle de la salle ou la Cour sera-t-elle amenée à faire son autocritique ?

Dans son rapport, M. Waelbroeck s'est attaché à définir deux types de tensions qui, selon lui, naissent de l'action de la Cour, les unes superficielles, les autres plus profondes. Les tensions qu'il qualifie de superficielles naîtraient de la difficulté rencontrée par les nouveaux Etats membres à « digérer » l'acquis communautaire. Personnellement, je me demande si le problème n'est pas plus profond et ne trouve pas ses racines dans une conception différente de la construction communautaire que se feraient certains nouveaux Etats membres. La jurisprudence de la Cour ferait naître, toujours selon M. Waelbroeck, des tensions plus profondes qui s'expliquent peut-être par le fait que les auteurs du traité avaient mal perçu l'ampleur du dessaisissement de pouvoirs qu'ils acceptaient, la portée de certaines règles et l'étendue de la compétence accordée à la Cour par l'effet combiné des dispositions des articles 169, 173 et 177 du traité. La conclusion de M. Waelbroeck a été que la Cour reste dans les limites du rôle qui lui a été imparti, en cherchant à empêcher la remise en cause de l'acquis communautaire.

M. Louis, pour sa part, nous a rappelé un certain nombre de situations dans lesquelles se sont révélées les résistances des Etats (Allemagne, France, Italie) ou même d'institutions communautaires. A cette occasion, il a examiné les résultats, tantôt positifs, tantôt négatifs, qu'avait eus l'intervention de la Cour.

Enfin, M. Vandersanden me semble avoir abordé la question des rapports entre la Cour et les Etats membres sous un angle plus politique, n'hésitant pas à évoquer ce que j'appellerai « les arrêts politiques », notamment en matière de taxes et mesures d'effet équivalent et en matière de politique agricole commune.

Notre débat pourrait porter tout d'abord sur la question fondamentale et générale du rôle de la Cour. En veillant au maintien et à l'élargissement de l'acquis communautaire, la Cour a-t-elle fait ce que l'on était en droit d'attendre d'elle ou, au contraire, est-elle allée trop loin ? Conviendrait-il de marquer un temps d'arrêt ? Les résistances politiques des Etats sont-elles ou non justifiées ? Nous pourrions par la suite examiner certains problèmes spécifiques soulevés par les rapports.

M. LAGRANGE

Au début de son exposé, M. Ryziger semblait souhaiter une mise en accusation de la Cour de façon à ce qu'elle ne soit point obligée de faire son autocritique. Je vais me permettre d'indiquer, d'ailleurs en toute simplicité, toute amitié et toute franchise, ce que je pense de l'évolution de sa jurisprudence.

En général, mais peut-être est-ce une déformation corporative, si j'ose dire, je suis d'accord avec les commissaires du gouvernement du Conseil d'Etat quand ils se prononcent contre leur juge et je suis d'accord avec les avocats généraux de la Cour quand celle-ci ne les suit pas !

Je voudrais surtout m'attacher à la théorie de l'applicabilité directe. Je crois qu'on ne louera jamais assez les premières orientations de la jurisprudence de la Cour et l'arrêt *Van Gend en Loos* qui fut décisif quant au choix des méthodes d'interprétation du traité dans un sens large, progressif.

Ainsi que je l'ai souvent écrit et dit, la Cour est une institution de la Communauté qui doit, dans la mesure de ses attributions, participer à l'élaboration de la Communauté et au fonctionnement de celle-ci.

Il y eut ensuite des développements qui furent non moins remarquables mais, personnellement, je trouve que la Cour a été trop loin en ce qui concerne le problème de l'applicabilité directe. Je pense plus particulièrement à l'arrêt *Charmasson*.

Pour ce qui me concerne, en tant qu'ancien membre du Conseil d'Etat français où j'ai fait toute ma carrière, le problème de l'applicabilité directe du droit communautaire doit être vu de la même façon que dans le cadre du droit national. Autrement dit, les dispositions du traité peuvent être directement applicables, de même que, dans le cadre national, une loi peut être directement applicable même lorsqu'elle prévoit des règlements d'application, mais à condition que l'application, en attendant l'intervention de ces règlements, soit possible.

C'était le cas, par exemple, dans l'arrêt *Reyners*. L'avocat néerlandais établi en Belgique remplissait toutes les conditions, sauf celle de la nationalité, pour exercer son activité en Belgique. Par application directe du traité, il avait le droit d'exercer cette activité en Belgique puisqu'aucune mesure d'application n'était nécessaire.

Dans l'arrêt *Charmasson,* la Cour a été plus loin. Il s'agissait de savoir ce qui se passait lorsque le traité avait prévu que des règlements d'application devaient être pris durant une période transitoire et que ces règlements n'avaient point été adoptés. La Cour décida — je simplifie un peu — que si aucun règlement n'avait été pris dans les délais prévus, le traité devenait directement applicable à l'expiration de ces délais.

Je crois, personnellement, que lorsque l'on se trouve devant une situation où les principes d'un traité ne peuvent pas être appliqués sans que des mesures d'application soient prises et qu'elles ne l'ont point été dans les délais prévus, c'est aller très loin que de reconnaître à tout particulier le droit d'exiger l'application brutale de ces principes.

En ce qui concerne les derniers développements de la jurisprudence de la Cour relative aux rares hypothèses où une organisation nationale de marché en matière agricole n'a pas été remplacée par une organisation commune, comme elle aurait dû l'être, avant le 1er janvier 1978, l'article 60, paragraphe 2, de l'acte d'adhésion justifiait et permettait une position plus souple. Ainsi que l'a souligné l'avocat général Warner, il convient de conserver un sens à cette disposition. Celle-ci n'en a aucun si, ainsi que le soutient la Cour, les organisations nationales de marché disparaissaient de plein droit au 1er janvier 1970. L'acte d'adhésion avait prévu qu'elles resteraient en vigueur pendant un certain temps. Elles étaient donc licites, au moins tant qu'elles n'avaient pas été remplacées. Il y avait d'autres arguments, mais je ne reviens pas sur les explications très claires qui nous ont été données tout à l'heure.

Les résultats de cette jurisprudence — je pense plus particulièrement à la guerre du mouton — ont beaucoup d'échos en France et je trouve cela regrettable. A l'origine de ces difficultés, il y a une certaine différence d'appréhension du droit communautaire par les tribunaux nationaux d'une part, qui sont naturellement imprégnés de leurs habitudes nationales, et par la Cour de justice d'autre part.

Personnellement, dès les premières conclusions que j'ai présentées sous le régime de la CECA, dans l'affaire dite des barèmes, j'ai défendu la thèse d'après laquelle on doit interpréter une disposition du traité en fonction de son contexte, de sa place dans le chapitre où elle se trouve, de la place du chapitre dans l'ensemble du traité. Cette méthode d'interprétation est normale dans un traité-loi comme le traité CECA.

Le traité du Marché commun est un peu plus souple, souvent un peu plus vague, en raison de son objet plus général, mais les principes sont les mêmes. On ne saurait tenir compte de travaux préparatoires qui n'ont pas été publiés. Il ne s'agit évidemment pas d'oublier complètement les buts et les objectifs du Marché commun en général et de la construction européenne qui doit l'accompagner. Mais, pour interpréter un texte, il est indispensable de raisonner conformément à ce texte et aux conditions dans lesquelles ce texte a été adopté et inséré dans l'ensemble dans lequel il figure.

La Cour de justice, quant à elle, a des théories que j'admire sans toujours très bien les comprendre : théorie de la finalité, de l'effet utile chère à mon voisin et ami Pescatore. L'effet utile, pour un juriste français, cela laisse un peu rêveur. Qu'est-ce que l'effet utile ? Je préfère personnellement la méthode que j'ai brièvement exposée. La jurisprudence actuelle de la Cour concernant l'applicabilité directe est trop large d'autant plus qu'elle peut s'appliquer aisément aux directives.

Je trouve que c'est regrettable et que si les avocats généraux de la Cour et les commissaires du gouvernement du Conseil d'Etat avaient pu dire le droit, nous n'aurions sans doute pas la guerre du mouton.

M. RYZIGER, *président*

M. Lagrange, qui fut pourtant très progressiste en son temps, semble trouver que le progrès a marché trop vite. C'est la méthode d'interprétation de la Cour qui est ici en cause et M. Lagrange serait en somme partisan, si j'ai bien compris, d'une interprétation plus exégétique du traité basée certes sur l'intention des rédacteurs, mais l'intention supposée à travers les textes.

Il s'oppose ainsi à la méthode de la Cour qui, souvent, lorsqu'il y a un vide juridique, recherche le fond commun des droits nationaux, ce qui est une autre méthode qu'on peut qualifier de téléologique ; c'est pourtant ainsi qu'a été créé un véritable droit communautaire.

M. LAGRANGE, interrompant l'orateur :

C'est ce que, pour ma part, j'ai toujours fait.

M. RYZIGER, *président*

M. Lagrange s'est élevé contre certaines notions, telles que celle de l'effet utile.

Cette notion d'effet utile peut être étrangère à certains juristes de la Communauté ; c'est peut-être notre cas. Mais cette notion peut, me semble-t-il, être puisée dans d'autres droits. Le droit français n'est pas le seul système juridique existant dans la Communauté et, personnellement, je pense que l'approche de la Cour peut précisément être qualifiée d'approche communautaire du droit.

Madame CUVELLIEZ

Il me semble que nous ne sommes pas suffisamment informés pour porter une appréciation sur le corps de jurisprudence de la Cour de justice.

Si j'ai bien compris, M. Waelbroeck était un peu étonné des inventions jurisprudentielles de la Cour, ou en tout cas il comprenait qu'on s'étonnât de celles-ci. Je voudrais dire que c'est un phénomène que nous connaissons dans nos ordres nationaux. Il n'y a donc pas lieu, me semble-t-il, de s'étonner.

M. Vandersanden a très justement dit qu'il examinait la jurisprudence de la Cour dans la dialectique « Etats membres, Cour de justice ». Mais s'il est vrai qu'il y a un ordre juridique de la Communauté, il me semble qu'il y a d'autres parties prenantes à cet ordre juridique que les Etats. Ce sont les personnes, les individus comme tels. Si l'on avait choisi comme thème de recherche : « les personnes et la jurisprudence de la Cour de justice », j'ai l'impression que ces qualificatifs de « hardi », d'« audacieux » ne seraient pas revenus au cours de cet après-midi avec la même répétition que le principe de l'acte clair, cher au Conseil d'Etat de France.

Je crois donc qu'avant de porter un jugement sur le rôle joué par la Cour, il faut aborder une autre dialectique.

Si l'on analyse la jurisprudence de la Cour dans l'arrêt *Reyners,* on constate qu'elle comporte un élément de progrès important mais à incidence économique très relative. Pour ce qui est de la sécurité sociale, on se trouve dans un domaine où les systèmes de sécurité sociale entre les différents pays ne sont pas à ce point divergents qu'on ne puisse appliquer avec une certaine efficacité le principe d'égalité de traitement. La Cour de justice veille effectivement à ce qu'au niveau communautaire ce principe soit respecté.

Au niveau des personnes, la Cour de justice est parfois restrictive. C'est le cas dans les affaires *Defrenne* qui portaient sur l'égalité entre les hommes et les femmes. Dans le premier arrêt concernant l'article 119, la Cour n'a pas accueilli la demande de la requérante ; elle a accepté une définition restrictive de la notion de rémunération. Dans le deuxième arrêt, elle a admis l'applicabilité directe de l'article 119 mais en y apportant d'importantes restrictions. Le troisième arrêt portant sur l'égalité de traitement a également rejeté la thèse de la requérante, de sorte que l'égalité de traitement n'apparaît pas comme un principe général du droit européen.

Si nous nous plaçons dans la dialectique « Cour de justice, individus », nous aurons une opinion différente sur la jurisprudence de la Cour de justice qui ne nous paraîtra pas audacieuse. Il ne faudrait pas que les éminents magistrats qui sont ici croient qu'ils manient avec vigueur le rouge et le noir.

Ils restent très sagement, très pragmatiquement, dans le système de rapport existant des forces économiques et ne bouleversent nullement ce rapport de forces.

M. Hjalte RASMUSSEN

In practice, we can say that our discussion about the Court is whether the Court is too little connected with the political world. But you were proposing to discuss whether the Court has been transgressing his role and I think that one should put a preliminary question in before that.

Transgressing its role compared to what?

If you look at the role of the Court with the eyes of a British lawyer, he would certainly say that it is useful that the Court should have the power to do this, every day. If you look at it with a Danish lawyer's eyes, he will normally say that the Court is doing too much in terms of political action. If you look at it with the eyes of an American accustomed to the U.S. Supreme Court, he will certainly in many cases say that it is a very timid Court.

So I think that we should do a little effort to define in what respect, compared to what we are talking about the Court's political action.

The Commission is a political animal and the Council is a political animal and I think that the Court is one too. One should consider the Court's role in the context of Community life and particularly I think one should think about the Court's action compared to courts in other federal contexts —you must not put too much attention on the words I use.

Compared to the U.S. Supreme Court one may come to conclusions that this European Court is only doing what it was supposed to do. Its mission is simply to give life to political compromises and to political doctrines which have been written into words which have, in turn, to be interpreted and explained by a court, and that is the way it is.

So one should not, I think, hesitate too much vis-à-vis the role of the Court and criticize it for being political. There is no misuse of power; the Court is merely acting, I think, as a normal federal supreme court. So I would propose to put the question rather in these terms: not *whether* the Court is politically acting—it ought to be so—but *how often* the Court should act politically and with how intense political decisions it should intervene in the life of the member states.

M. ALEXANDER

Le professeur Rasmussen a raison de souligner que toute évaluation de la jurisprudence de la Cour est relative.

M. Waelbroeck, dans la première partie de son exposé, a envisagé la jurisprudence de la Cour dans l'optique des critiques des Etats membres, qui se voyaient dessaisis de pouvoirs qu'ils ne pensaient pas avoir transférés et il a essayé d'apprécier si cette critique était justifiée. Il a dressé un tableau montrant une évolution constante dans le sens d'un accroissement du champ d'application du traité.

Je ne suis pas tout à fait d'accord avec ce tableau. Je ne suis pas non plus tout à fait d'accord avec ce que M. Louis a ajouté lorsqu'il a dit que la Cour, dans sa jurisprudence, était ferme sur les principes mais admettait des aménagements pragmatiques.

Jusqu'il y a peu, j'étais un juriste européen, fier et satisfait d'un édifice judiciaire clair, hardi, avec des contours très exacts. La récente jurisprudence de la Cour m'amène à réviser mon opinion.

A titre d'exemple, je vais comparer certains arrêts anciens avec des arrêts plus récents.

Dans l'arrêt *Dassonville,* la Cour avait jugé que l'exigence par la Belgique d'un certificat d'authenticité, plus difficilement accessible aux importateurs de whisky régulièrement en libre pratique en France qu'aux importateurs du même produit en provenance directe du Royaume-Uni, constituait une mesure d'effet équivalant à une restriction quantitative. La Belgique n'ayant pas, de l'avis de la Commission, mis fin à l'infraction ainsi constatée, la Commission a engagé la procédure de l'article 169. Je ne vous cache pas ma surprise de lire dans le deuxième arrêt, qui en est résulté, que la Belgique n'avait pas violé le traité, que tout le monde — en tout cas la Commission et, je dois l'avouer, moi-même — avait mal compris le critère décisif contenu dans le premier arrêt ; que ce qui comptait, c'était de savoir si les formalités que la Belgique impose aux importateurs indirects étaient déraisonnables par rapport à celles qu'elle impose à l'importateur direct.

Autre exemple : il y a quelques années, l'arrêt *Van Haaster* nous apprenait qu'une restriction à la production pouvait, à cause de ses effets, constituer une mesure d'effet équivalant à une interdiction d'exportation. Or, il y a quelques mois, la Cour a estimé qu'une restriction qui — cela ressort clairement de l'exposé des motifs — visait vraiment à rendre impossible l'exportation de produits de charcuterie contenant de la viande chevaline, ne constituait pas une mesure d'effet équivalent [1].

Je ne pense donc pas qu'il s'agisse simplement d'aménagements pragmatiques apportés à la doctrine de la Cour. Je me demande s'il n'y a pas un flux et un reflux de cette même doctrine.

(1) Arrêt *Groenveld* du 8 novembre 1979, aff. 15/79, *Rec.*, 1979, p. 3409.

M. GLAESNER

Je voudrais faire quelques observations à propos de l'intervention de M. l'avocat général Lagrange. Je vais essayer d'apprécier si la Cour est allée trop loin en partant du texte des traités.

Si l'on examine les dispositions du traité, il apparaît que la Cour a été chargée d'assurer la protection des individus vis-à-vis des décisions des autorités de la Communauté. Il s'agit là de la contrepartie normale de l'applicabilité directe des actes communautaires à ces mêmes particuliers. Dans l'exercice de ces pouvoirs, je ne trouve guère d'éléments politiques. La Cour agit là comme une Cour de cassation, d'une haute qualité.

Cependant, les traités eux-mêmes ont confié des tâches politiques à la Cour. D'une part, ils en ont fait une Cour constitutionnelle, compétente pour trancher les conflits entre les institutions de la Communauté, aspect rarement réalisé, ainsi que les conflits entre la Communauté et les Etats membres ou encore les conflits entre les Etats membres et relatifs à l'application des traités. La Cour étant dès lors une Cour constitutionnelle, on ne saurait nier l'élément politique qui est attaché à toute cour de ce type. D'autre part, la Cour s'est vu confier également une tâche particulière. Aux termes de l'article 177, elle a l'obligation de veiller à ce que l'application du droit communautaire par les tribunaux nationaux soit uniforme.

Bien sûr, le fait que la Cour exerce un pouvoir qui a un impact politique n'empêche pas que l'on puisse discuter ses décisions. Il faut cependant être conscient que la Cour, en exerçant ses pouvoirs, risque des conflits avec les Etats. Cela est inévitable et je suis sûr que la Cour a chaque fois mesuré l'impact que le développement du droit communautaire lié à sa jurisprudence pouvait avoir sur la situation politique dans la Communauté dans le sens large du mot.

Je vous rappelle que la politique est l'art du possible et que, dans ce contexte-là, la Cour doit naviguer en utilisant les instruments juridiques à sa disposition. Ce n'est pas toujours facile.

M. BRÜCKNER

Mes observations porteront plus spécialement sur la résistance des Etats membres à reconnaître la jurisprudence de la Cour et, d'autre part, sur « l'irréalisme de la Cour ».

Il est vrai que l'impact de l'arrêt *AETR* ne s'est manifesté que progressivement et lentement. Mais je crois que, dans l'exposé de M. Louis notamment, on a peut-être méconnu l'importance de l'environnement international dans lequel se déroulent les activités internationales des Etats membres et de la Communauté.

A ce propos, il est important de noter que la Communauté n'est pas membre de l'ONU ni des organisations qui relèvent de la famille de l'ONU. Ces organisations ne sont pas susceptibles de reconnaître la Communauté comme membre à part entière sur le même pied que les Etats. Cela vaut également — au moins en partie — pour les conférences internationales, par exemple les conférences sur la pêche où la Communauté a eu les plus grandes difficultés à se faire reconnaître. Un problème analogue se pose dans les relations avec les pays de l'Est.

A mon avis. il convient de souligner que la résistance des Etats membres n'est pas aussi forte que l'on croit. Il faut en effet noter qu'en dépit des difficultés rencontrées au niveau international, la jurisprudence *AETR* a été appliquée dans l'accord de pêche avec les Etats-Unis, dans la participation de la Communauté à l'accord international sur la pêche dans l'Atlantique du Nord-Ouest, dans la convention sur les animaux dans les élevages et le *codex alimentarius* sur les sucres. Il existe encore d'autres conventions qui sont en voie de préparation.

Je voudrais également dire que la Cour n'est pas aussi irréaliste qu'on le prétend. Dans l'arrêt *AETR,* elle a prévu une procédure de délégation aux Etats membres dans les cas où il y a une impossibilité sur la scène internationale d'assurer la participation de la Communauté. Dans l'avis 1/78, d'autre part, elle a reconnu la pratique des accords mixtes.

Enfin, aussi longtemps qu'en droit international il n'existe pas encore un « principe de succession » généralement reconnu, il faut, pour faire reconnaître la Communauté comme sujet de droit international, tenir compte également de l'attitude des pays tiers et des règles du jeu telles qu'elles résultent des statuts des organisations et des conférences internationales déjà existantes.

M. MERTENS de WILMARS

Tout d'abord, j'ai toujours des hésitations quand j'entends parler d'une éventuelle activité politique de la Cour. J'ai vraiment l'impression que le problème est mal posé.

Il va de soi qu'une juridiction comme la nôtre — et ce que j'en dis est vrai pour toutes les juridictions — est, jour après jour, confrontée avec des problèmes juridiques qui ont des implications politiques. Dans les Etats membres, il n'y a aucun juge, qu'il soit civil ou pénal, qui ne se soit trouvé dans la même situation. Ce n'est pas parce que l'on tranche un problème à implications politiques, suivant les règles juridiques que l'on estime être applicables, que l'on peut être « accusé » de faire de la politique. Je crois que cela doit être dit très clairement.

Ma seconde observation est la suivante. Il doit également être dit clairement que la Cour se considère, lorsqu'elle exécute la mission que lui confie le traité, comme la gardienne d'un droit créateur d'un équilibre entre les Etats membres et la Communauté. Il est du devoir de la Cour de protéger cet équilibre, aussi bien lorsqu'il est menacé aux dépens des Etats que lorsqu'il l'est aux dépens des institutions communautaires.

On reconnaîtra cependant que, dans la première phase du développement d'une organisation comme celle des Communautés européennes, c'est plutôt le maintien des compétences transférées aux institutions qui requiert une vigilance particulière.

Mais — et je remercie le professeur Louis de l'avoir fait observer — on peut trouver dans la jurisprudence de la Cour de justice des indications de plus en plus fréquentes relatives à la préoccupation de la Cour de justice de ménager également l'équilibre des compétences dans le sens de la sauvegarde des compétences des Etats membres. Les expressions choisies par M. Louis, qui parlait de question de principe lorsqu'il s'agissait de conforter l'édifice communautaire et de questions pragmatiques, lorsqu'il s'agissait de reconnaître les droits des Etats membres, ne me paraissent pas tout à fait adéquates. Dans l'un comme dans l'autre cas, c'est la sauvegarde de l'équilibre institutionnel qui est en jeu. Cette préoccupation est présente dans la jurisprudence de la Cour de justice.

CONCLUSIONS

par

Christian TOMUSCHAT,

Professeur à l'Université de Bonn

Mesdames,
Messieurs,

Les organisateurs de cette journée d'études m'ont confié la tâche de tirer les conclusions de la journée. Je ne puis évidemment résumer toutes ces contributions si brillantes, si claires, si denses. Je tâcherai seulement de dégager les éléments primordiaux du débat.

Premièrement, il me semble qu'on est arrivé, après presque trente ans d'activité de la Cour, à un moment historique. La Cour a consolidé son autorité lentement mais progressivement ; aujourd'hui, cependant, on arrive à une situation où une certaine résistance de la part des Etats se manifeste. Cette résistance se comprend fort bien maintenant que l'on découvre, d'une part, toute l'étendue des pouvoirs de la Communauté et, d'autre part, l'étendue des pouvoirs que les Etats membres ont perdus. La révolte paraît donc inévitable.

Il me semble que c'est dans l'œuvre de la Cour que ce processus de communautarisation trouve son expression la plus tangible. On a souvent dit que la Commission était disciplinée. On a même affirmé que la Commission avait été dégradée au rang d'un secrétariat du Conseil des ministres. C'est un jugement que, personnellement, je ne partage pas. Mais personne n'a encore osé soutenir que la Cour avait été dégradée au rang d'un simple tribunal servant les intérêts des Etats membres pris individuellement.

La Cour a gardé sa vigueur primitive et l'admiration pour l'œuvre de la Cour est grande. On a parlé aujourd'hui de la hardiesse de sa jurisprudence qui, dans un passé récent, a souvent été critiquée. Au cours de cette journée, certains orateurs ont nuancé cette appréciation en faisant remarquer que, depuis peu, la Cour semblait revenir en arrière dans certains domaines.

Permettez-moi de jeter encore un regard assez bref sur les trois grands thèmes qui ont été examinés au cours de nos travaux.

Tout d'abord, le premier thème à l'ordre du jour était : *Les Etats membres, les juges et la procédure*. Pour ce qui est de la structure institutionnelle de la Cour, le professeur Jacobs a souligné à juste titre qu'il n'y a pas de contradiction entre les deux étiquettes de « cour supranationale » et de « cour représentative ». Il faut que la Cour combine les deux éléments pour être une institution acceptée par les Etats membres.

M. Jacobs a eu le mérite d'articuler en des questions précises les soucis qu'il nous a exposés.

Sa première remarque concernant l'origine des juges — origine nationale ou origine de *law districts* (circonscriptions légales) — n'a pas trouvé un écho très favorable puisqu'elle aboutirait à confier un avantage à la Grande-Bretagne. Il est toutefois possible que d'autres pays à structure régionale aient l'orgueil de présenter eux aussi plusieurs juges. Il y aurait donc là une évolution assez incertaine.

En ce qui concerne la durée du mandat des juges, nous n'avons pas assez approfondi la problématique. M. Jacobs a insisté tout particulièrement sur la courte durée du mandat qui est seulement de six ans. Bien qu'il n'y ait pas eu d'abus visible dans le passé, on peut très bien se poser la question de savoir s'il ne faudrait pas suivre l'exemple de la Cour constitutionnelle allemande dont les juges siègent pendant douze ans avec un mandat qui n'est pas renouvelable.

La question des opinions individuelles trouve une réponse assez nette. Personne dans cette salle ne s'est prononcé pour l'admission de telles opinions individuelles. Nous avons tous présent à l'esprit les excès résultant de la pratique des opinions individuelles que l'on rencontre à la Cour internationale de justice où les décisions de la Cour elle-même sont souvent submergées par les observations des différents juges.

M. Jacobs a eu tout à fait raison de se demander si des chambres composées de trois juges seulement possèdent encore un caractère représentatif. En effet, il ne faut pas oublier que c'est l'un des principes traditionnels, lorsqu'il y a une juridiction internationale, que chaque Etat partie ait « son » juge au sein de cette instance. Il faut donc procéder d'une façon extrêmement prudente. Il est vrai, cependant, comme M. Glaesner l'a souligné, que, dans bien des cas, on ne pourrait pas déterminer quel serait l'Etat national ayant droit un nommer un juge *ad hoc*, parce que de nombreux litiges n'ont pas un caractère proprement national.

En ce qui concerne la procédure de l'article 177, le professeur Jacobs, se basant sur un mémoire de la Grande-Bretagne, a posé la question de savoir si le délai de deux mois est suffisant pour examiner en profondeur tous les arguments qui peuvent être en cause. Sur ce point, des précisions très importantes ont été apportées par MM. les juges ici présents qui ont souligné que, de plus en plus, la Cour adopte une attitude active en posant des questions aux parties. Il y a un consensus général, parmi les participants à cette journée d'études, que cette pratique pourrait encore être renforcée pour aboutir à un « Rechtsgespräch », comme l'avait préconisé il y a longtemps déjà le grand juriste Adolf Arndt. Critiquant la Cour constitutionnelle allemande, il avait dit que, devant une telle enceinte, il était incompatible avec la dignité des parties de les réduire au seul objet de la procédure et qu'il fallait donc leur accorder la possibilité de développer leurs arguments sur les points considérés comme pertinents par les juges.

Il a été souligné que le rapport d'audience, qui énumère les arguments des parties, permet aux plaideurs d'être parfaitement instruits de toute l'ampleur du débat.

En ce qui concerne le deuxième thème : *Les Etats membres et les compétences de la Cour,* le professeur Kovar nous a fait un exposé très complet dont le premier volet était axé sur la garantie de l'autonomie de la Communauté. M. Kovar a attiré l'attention sur la formulation insuffisante de l'article 177 dont le texte pourrait permettre à des instances juridictionnelles inférieures d'apprécier elles-mêmes la validité d'un acte communautaire. Nous sommes parvenus sur ce point à un consensus très remarquable. Toutes les interventions ont fait remarquer que le seul choix ouvert à une instance juridictionnelle inférieure était soit de reconnaître la validité de l'acte communautaire, soit de saisir la Cour de justice, l'instance nationale ne pouvant pas elle-même déclarer l'invalidité de l'acte communautaire.

En ce qui concerne la procédure de l'article 177, nous avons été influencés par les événements que nous connaissons tous. M. Puissochet nous a conseillé de miser sur la confiance mutuelle, qui, toutefois, fait manifestement défaut. Les raisons en sont patentes. En effet, M. le conseiller Lagrange a reconnu que le Conseil d'Etat de France n'applique plus la théorie de l'acte clair dans le sens original défini par Laférière et qu'il en a profondément modifié la teneur. Je partage sur ce point les craintes et les critiques qui ont été exprimées avec une vigueur particulière par M. Ryziger.

Est-il possible de remédier à cette situation ? Le professeur Kovar nous a rappelé certaines propositions : instaurer un droit de recours des particuliers, créer un recours dans l'intérêt de la loi. Il nous a mis en garde car ces propositions introduiraient un élément de hiérarchisation, de subordination alors que, actuellement, le système est vraiment axé sur la confiance mutuelle, la coopération.

Le deuxième volet était consacré au contrôle de la légalité. Faut-il renforcer l'article 169 ? M. Kovar a eu raison de nous rappeler que même les tribunaux n'échappent pas à la règle générale selon laquelle l'Etat est responsable de tous ses organes, de ses tribunaux comme de son parlement. Il était extrêmement utile que M. Pescatore attire notre attention sur deux arrêts où la Cour a laissé entrevoir que la procédure de l'article 169 est plus qu'une procédure en constatation, la Cour ayant certaines possibilités de prendre des mesures plus concrètes.

M. Barav a douté un peu de ces possibilités d'action et M. Paulin, finalement, a posé la question de savoir si un Etat, qui ne respecte pas un arrêt de la Cour, peut encourir une responsabilité pécuniaire. Personnellement, je suis convaincu que le fait qu'un Etat ne respecte pas un arrêt de la Cour de justice est un acte illicite du point de vue du droit international. Il reste cependant à déterminer si un tel recours entre dans le cadre de l'article 170 ou bien si cet article permet seulement d'obtenir une constatation du manquement, comme c'est le cas pour l'article 169. Je crois que le sujet devrait encore être approfondi et qu'il ne nous est pas possible aujourd'hui de donner une réponse définitive.

Nous avons abordé une autre question, celle de savoir si un recours contre les actes du Parlement européen et du Conseil européen était possible. Nous aurions peut-être pu l'approfondir. A mon avis, lorsque le Conseil européen fait usage des pouvoirs conférés par le traité au Conseil des ministres, lorsqu'il émet un acte faisant grief, la procédure normale est applicable. L'acte du Conseil européen est un acte attaquable.

Le troisième grand thème : *les Etats membres et la jurisprudence de la Cour* a été développé d'une façon magistrale par MM. les professeurs Louis, Vandersanden et Waelbroeck.

M. Waelbroeck a rappelé deux grandes difficultés. La première, c'est que les Etats se sont dessaisis irrévocablement de certains pouvoirs. Il peut y avoir maintenant certains regrets qui se manifestent par des actes qu'il ne faut peut-être pas prendre trop au sérieux. L'histoire nous apprend qu'il y a eu des tensions et des frictions dans toutes les structures fédérales et confédérales. Il serait surprenant qu'il en aille autrement pour les Communautés.

La deuxième difficulté, c'est que les traités communautaires sont vraiment des textes dynamiques. C'est du *law in action*. Evidemment, les traités ne sont plus ce qu'ils furent au début de l'existence de la Communauté. Il faut maintenant les lire à la lumière des arrêts de la Cour. Je crois que c'est tout à fait normal. Beaucoup d'orateurs nous ont d'ailleurs rappelé que la Cour fait œuvre de juridiction constitutionnelle, ce qui est vu avec méfiance dans les pays qui ne disposent pas d'une cour constitutionnelle, où l'on admet difficilement qu'une cour puisse se prononcer pratiquement sur toutes les questions en relation avec l'interprétation de l'instrument de base de la Communauté.

Le professeur Louis a décrit les résistances qui s'opposent à la jurisprudence de la Cour. Elles sont normales de la part de cours suprêmes qui n'avaient pas l'habitude d'être contrôlées. Le Conseil d'Etat français n'est pas le seul à s'être rebellé. La Cour constitutionnelle allemande s'est élevée contre la jurisprudence de la Cour en matière de droits de l'homme. On peut savoir gré au professeur Louis d'avoir rappelé que la Cour de Karlsruhe semble décidée à abandonner la jurisprudence inaugurée en 1974.

Il était aussi très judicieux de nous indiquer les tensions qui se manifestent dans le domaine des relations extérieures et surtout dans le domaine de la coopération, où la Communauté n'a pas pu occuper toutes les positions qu'elle était en droit d'occuper d'après la jurisprudence de la Cour de justice. M. Brückner nous a rappelé les difficultés provenant des statuts des organisations internationales qui prévoient comme membres seulement les Etats.

Enfin, il me semble qu'il était extrêmement utile que l'on n'ait pas seulement parlé de la hardiesse, mais aussi de la timidité de la Cour. Il est tout particulièrement réconfortant pour les juges ici présents que des orateurs aient dit que la Cour devrait faire preuve de beaucoup plus de hardiesse, surtout dans le domaine social.

J'ai résumé très brièvement, très sommairement, je le reconnais, les principaux arguments qui ont été avancés au cours de la discussion. Permettez-moi une remarque finale. En tout cas, l'admiration pour le travail de la Cour s'est manifestée tout au long de cette journée. Rien de révolutionnaire n'a été proposé ; toutes les propositions ne concernent que certains aménagements mineurs du Statut de la Cour. Personne n'a vraiment contesté la jurisprudence de la Cour.

Il convient maintenant de rétablir la confiance. C'est peut-être la tâche la plus importante. La Communauté n'est pas encore un empire éclaté !

ALLOCUTION DE CLOTURE

par

Paul FORIERS,

Président de l'Institut d'Etudes européennes,
Professeur à l'Université libre de Bruxelles

Mesdames,

Messieurs,

Nous voilà au terme d'une journée passionnante où la dialectique de la Cour de justice et des Etats membres a été au centre du débat.

La problématique ne fut pas seulement juridique, ce que l'intitulé des thèmes traités aurait pu faire croire ; elle fut aussi politique, non pas au sens courant du vocable — marqué aujourd'hui d'une certaine connotation péjorative — mais au sens le plus élevé du terme.

Elle devait nécessairement comporter ce double caractère, car aussi bien l'Europe des Juges allait fatalement rencontrer chemin faisant des résistances de la part des Etats membres, alors que la Cour, pour construire cette Europe, exerçait en toute indépendance sa mission.

En cela d'ailleurs, cette résistance n'est pas singulière, elle s'inscrit dans un processus qui n'a nulle spécificité. Songeons, par exemple, aux réactions des entreprises, également sujets de droit de la Communauté, à certains arrêts de la Cour et cette attitude n'est-elle pas l'expression d'une même tendance ?

« Le recours du Conseil et du Conseil européen à des actes innommés plutôt qu'aux catégories d'actes dont l'article 189 du traité CEE définit la portée est révélateur des tentatives faites par les gouvernements pour échapper au carcan des contraintes juridiques dans les domaines où ils veulent conserver leur liberté d'action » que relevaient si opportunément Jean-Victor Louis, Georges Vandersanden et Michel Waelbroeck dans leur commun et d'ailleurs lumineux rapport n'a-t-il pas son homologue dans les pratiques des opérateurs économiques eux aussi soucieux d'échapper à ce collier de fer ? Rien, dès lors, qui doive surprendre.

Comment pourtant expliquer cette attitude dans le chef des Etats dont on aurait pu croire que, par-delà le politique, ils se sentiraient inconditionnellement liés ?

Peut-être, tout compte fait et fort simplement, par le fait que ces Etats sont intégrés en tant que sujets dans une *Communauté* et qu'ayant pris conscience de ce phénomène qui n'est pourtant que la conséquence logique de leur volonté, ils cherchent à en éviter toutes les conséquences.

« Chaque Etat a ses lois, qu'il tient de sa nature ou qu'il change à son choix », disait Voltaire.

Je ne pense pas que l'Etat, en tant qu'entité concrète, croie encore qu'il existe des lois qui tiennent à sa nature, mais certainement il est convaincu qu'il peut toujours changer les lois à son choix. C'est que les Etats, même fondamentalement démocratiques, ne sont guère habitués « à devoir se soumettre aux décisions d'une volonté juridiquement distincte de la leur propre » pour reprendre la pertinente expression de Guy Herraud.

Autre élément complémentaire : la Cour, par sa volonté de défendre sa mission institutionnelle avec intransigeance au sein d'une Communauté qui constitue un « Etat de droit », ce qui implique dans l'ordre européen « des règles contraignantes, uniformément applicables et protectrices des droits des personnes », prend fermement position dans la dialectique du *pouvoir* opposé au *citoyen* ou mieux encore à l'*individu*. Cette dialectique est perenne et son histoire est celle de tous les temps avec ses balancements, ses repentirs, ses choix, ses succès temporaires, ses échecs tout aussi fluctuants et partant alternés. Comment aurait-on pu, dès lors, éviter sinon l'affrontement tout au moins certaines contestations ?

Certes, pendant longtemps, la Cour a paru triompher. Le président Lecourt [1] pouvait naguère à juste titre écrire :

« L'effet direct était contesté ; il ne l'est plus. La primauté était niée ; elle est admise. Disparue aussi la double attitude de cet Etat qui résistait à l'effet direct du droit communautaire dans son pays, mais en réclamait ailleurs le bénéfice. On verrait enfin un des nouveaux Etats membres s'opposer d'abord, lui aussi, à l'effet direct d'une disposition du traité pour l'admettre dans les affaires suivantes après fixation de la jurisprudence ».

C'était là effectivement un bulletin de victoire qui paraissait fondé. Mais les victoires ne doivent pas faire oublier les épreuves qui en marquent la difficile conquête, ni le fait qu'elles peuvent être remises en question. Et c'est, dans une certaine mesure, ce qui arrive aujourd'hui.

Je ne me permettrais pas, même indirectement, de suggérer à la Cour de conserver son équanimité. Il est bon qu'elle ait la juste perception des réactions que son œuvre suscite. Mais de combien de facteurs de succès ne

(1) *L'Europe des Juges*, Bruxelles, 1976, p. 307 et 308.

dispose-t-elle pas ? Son indépendance, sa prudence, sa fermeté et surtout l'adhésion que son œuvre, malgré certains remous, emporte de la part d'une grande majorité des sujets de droit de la Communauté, convaincue du rôle qu'elle joue comme protecteur de l'être individuel et de sa personnalité.

En cela, elle s'est assurée, par sa jurisprudence et par-delà les textes, un très réel pouvoir fondé sur la force du faible si j'ose dire et qui lui vaut son soutien.

En étendant notamment le champ d'application territorial et matériel du traité, elle s'est concilié un large consensus emportant l'adhésion et, partant, légitimant et confortant son action par référence aux finalités humaines.

L'on a beaucoup insisté au cours de ces travaux sur la collaboration judiciaire entre la Cour de justice et les juges nationaux. Tout compte fait, cette collaboration dépasse nos espérances et cela aussi est un gage précieux d'avenir.

Les magistrats nationaux en tant qu'organes de l'Etat et juges de droit commun sont directement intégrés dans le processus communautaire et il est né entre eux et la Cour de justice une heureuse connivence, car ces magistrats se sentent approuvés dans leur action et valorisés dans leur propos.

L'arrêt *Simmenthal* a été commenté et glosé après avoir été scruté juridiquement avec des microscopes. Cela a donné des travaux d'une très grande qualité d'ailleurs, dont les observations de Barav ([2]) ne sont qu'un exemple topique.

Mais, vu sous un autre angle, n'est-il pas révélateur de l'appui que le juge national trouve auprès de la Cour ?

« Attendu (...) que le juge national a l'obligation d'assurer la protection des droits conférés par les dispositions de l'ordre juridique communautaire *sans qu'il ait à demander* ou *attendre* l'élimination effective par les organes nationaux habilités à cet effet, d'éventuelles mesures nationales qui feraient obstacle à l'applicabilité directe et immédiate des règles communautaires » (attendu 26 dudit arrêt).

Tout cela ne constitue-t-il pas pour le magistrat national le juste sentiment de son indépendance, de son rôle et de son pouvoir ? En l'espèce, la Cour ne laisse même pas la possibilité de mettre en œuvre la procédure d'inconstitutionnalité par les autorités nationales qui en ont la charge.

Que le gouvernement italien tenait pourtant à cette prérogative, voilà qui n'est pas douteux. Il était présent à l'instance et l'agent italien défendit

---

([2]) Les effets du droit communautaire directement applicable, *Cah. dr. eur.*, 1978, p. 260 et suiv.

avec intelligence et habileté sa thèse, mais son effort fut vain. Par contre, pour le Pretore de Susa quelle confirmation de ses prérogatives ! Il n'a, ni à demander l'élimination effective par les organes nationaux habilités à cet effet, ni à attendre que ces organes prennent une initiative quelconque. Quel rôle éminent est donc le sien !

Mais quittons ces considérations rhétoriques et sociologiques. Revenons au juridique.

L'on a beaucoup parlé de réformes utiles voire nécessaires, *de lege ferenda* somme toute, traduisant de la sorte implicitement une certaine hésitation sur le rôle possible de l'interprétation. Il est vrai que l'on n'hésite pas à dire que la Cour a déjà interprété le traité bien au-delà de ce que ses auteurs avaient envisagé.

Mais est-ce bien, sur le plan du droit, un reproche pertinent ? L'interprète ne se borne pas à expliquer ce que comporte le raccourci des textes, il adapte ceux-ci et donne nécessairement un sens nouveau à la règle plus ou moins ancienne, l'obscurcit peut-être, mais la féconde et, partant, crée finalement la règle nouvelle. Notre regretté collègue René Dekkers n'hésitait pas à écrire que l'interprète propose le droit nouveau et que sa tâche consiste à faire dire à la loi tout ce qui est possible et utile qu'elle dise « Quand bien même le législateur n'y aurait pas songé ».

Ce qui est vrai pour l'interprète sur le plan du droit national, peut-il devenir faux sur le plan du droit communautaire ?

La Cour assure le respect de la constitution communautaire, note Jean-Victor Louis (3), mais ce qui importe dans une constitution, comme dans toute loi d'ailleurs, c'est moins le respect de ce que ses auteurs avaient envisagé à l'origine que l'esprit qui se dégage de leur œuvre qui acquiert de ce fait une vie propre. L'esprit, c'est-à-dire l'idée centrale, maîtresse, le principe, l'objet essentiel que recouvrent les textes.

C'est ce qu'a fait la Cour de justice par le recours à une interprétation que je qualifierai d'éclectique, tant il est vrai qu'elle a mis en œuvre toutes les méthodes d'interprétation du droit international ou interne selon les circonstances et les espèces, mais cet éclectisme privilégie finalement l'interprétation systématique et téléologique, c'est-à-dire la structure et le but.

La Cour entend réaliser avec raison une politique juridique. L'article 177 du traité lui en donne notamment le moyen. En agissant de la sorte, elle agit en tant qu'institution et, comme toute institution, la Cour met en œuvre

---

(3) *L'Ordre juridique communautaire*, Bruxelles, 1979, Commission des Communautés européennes, n° 57, p. 45.

une idéologie c'est-à-dire une doctrine, des valeurs c'est-à-dire des pôles de référence et des techniques c'est-à-dire des procédés opératoires pour réaliser son dessein.

Or la doctrine est étonnamment constante malgré le renouvellement des hommes qui la composent et elle mérite d'être soutenue dans son effort. La Cour veut réaliser la nouvelle société que le traité annonce dans ses nouvelles dimensions et ses nouvelles structures. C'est là sa doctrine et elle n'entend point s'en départir, ce qui lui donne parfois des audaces singulières. L'arrêt *Continental Can,* dans l'énoncé de ses principes, en est un exemple obvie.

Personne ne peut, d'autre part, contester que la Cour ait élu des valeurs : l'égalité, la liberté, la solidarité, l'unité, l'utilité, l'efficacité. Ce sont ses pôles principaux de référence. Leur réalisation sur le plan pratique ne peut se concevoir sans une interprétation détachée de toute contrainte exégétique.

En tout cas, sa liberté d'interprète doit être d'autant plus grande qu'en tant qu'institution communautaire chargée d'assurer « la réalisation des tâches confiées à la Communauté », son rôle institutionnel ne se borne pas, comme l'écrivait avec toute l'autorité qui s'attache à ses opinions le Procureur général Ganshof van der Mersch, « à statuer sur des contestations et à interpréter dans ces limites le droit communautaire, mais aussi à participer à la poursuite de l'intégration européenne » (4).

Que ceci conforte la Cour dans ses initiatives.

J'ai dit que l'on avait beaucoup parlé de réformes *de lege ferenda,* mais Monsieur le Juge Pescatore avec cette claire vision des choses qui le caractérise a exprimé courageusement le sentiment que la plupart de nous conservions *in petto :* le caractère utopique de cette solution, utopique car l'utopie se caractérise par la négation ou tout au moins le télescopage du facteur temps et le fait qu'elle est la bouteille jetée à la mer.

Il arrive certes que le message soit finalement reçu et entendu, mais avons-nous le loisir d'attendre ?

Aussi, devons-nous, là où c'est possible, car je reconnais bien volontiers que ce ne l'est pas toujours, appuyer la Cour et l'aider à tracer avec une certaine audace la frontière entre la politique et le droit. En cela, nous avons un rôle à jouer. Oserait-on dire qu'il n'a pas été pleinement réalisé au cours

---

(4) L'ordre juridique des Communautés européennes et le droit international, *RCADI,* 1975, p. 267.

de cette rencontre grâce aux travaux de nos éminents rapporteurs et à la richesse de nos échanges de vues auxquels ont bien voulu participer deux des plus brillants membres de la Cour, Messieurs les Juges Mertens de Wilmars et Pescatore déjà cité.

Que tous trouvent ici l'expression de notre reconnaissance, comme Madame Charlier et son équipe, sans lesquelles rien de ce qui s'est fait aujourd'hui n'aurait pu être réalisé.

ANNEXES

I. LE FONCTIONNEMENT ACTUEL ET FUTUR DE LA COUR DE JUSTICE DES COMMUNAUTES EUROPEENNES *

(Europe Documents, n° 1034 du 20 décembre 1978*)*

Au moment où le « Comité des Sages » désigné par le Conseil Européen le 5 décembre entame ses réflexions au sujet d'un meilleur fonctionnement des mécanismes et des méthodes de travail des Institutions de la Communauté, il est intéressant de connaître le texte du Mémorandum que la Cour de Justice elle-même, en la personne de son président M. H. Kutscher, a adressé il y a quelque temps au président en exercice du Conseil M. Genscher « sur les mesures qu'elle juge nécessaires aux fins de son fonctionnement actuel et futur ».

Nous publions le texte intégral de ce Mémorandum, suivi du texte du communiqué que le Conseil (des ministres de la Justice) a rendu public le 9 octobre 1978, au sujet de ce Mémorandum, ainsi que deux autres extraits dudit communiqué, concernant la création (future) d'un tribunal pour litiges entre les institutions et leur personnel, et d'une déclaration sur la connaissance du droit communautaire.

A. MEMORANDUM DE LA COUR SUR LES MESURES QU'ELLE JUGE NECESSAIRES AUX FINS DE SON FONCTIONNEMENT ACTUEL ET FUTUR

1. LES DONNEES DU PROBLEME.

1. Le volume des affaires dont la Cour est saisie marque un accroissement constant et de plus en plus rapide. Il est ainsi d'ores et déjà en train de dépasser l'extrême limite de ce qu'il paraît possible d'accomplir au moyen des effectifs dont la Cour dispose à présent, et sur la base de la réglementation actuelle. Dans cet ordre d'idées, la Cour se permet de rappeler qu'elles s'est toujours efforcée — et, pense-t-elle, jusqu'à présent avec succès — de maintenir la durée des procédures dans des limites raisonnables, soit en moyenne sept mois pour les affaires préjudicielles et 12 à 18 mois pour les recours directs. Dans ces conditions, la Cour a pu éviter jusqu'ici des arriérés judiciaires.

On trouvera en annexe quelques chiffres qui parlent d'eux-mêmes.

2. Les demandes exposées dans le présent mémorandum tiennent compte, en outre, de deux autres facteurs:

a) L'adhésion à la Communauté de la Grèce, du Portugal et de l'Espagne aura nécessairement des répercussions sur la composition, l'organisation et le fonctionnement de la Cour.

Sur la base des informations dont elle dispose, la Cour part de la prémisse selon laquelle l'adhésion de la Grèce deviendrait effective vers la fin de 1980 ou pendant le premier semestre de 1981, alors que celle du Portugal et de l'Espagne se situerait plutôt vers 1984, sans qu'il soit à présent certain si ces deux pays deviendront membres de la Communauté en même temps ou successivement.

b) Dans un avenir prévisible, plusieurs Conventions passées entre les Etats membres et attribuant des compétences à la Cour entreront en vigueur. Parmi elles, il faut mentionner notamment la Convention sur le brevet communautaire. Selon les prévisions actuellement possibles, il est permis de penser que la Cour n'assumera qu'à partir de 1984 la plénitude des charges que lui impose cette Convention; en tout cas, il apparaît hautement probable que celle-ci aura alors pour effet de multiplier le nombre des affaires introduites devant la Cour.

---

* NDLR : les organisateurs de la journée d'études remercient la rédaction du Bulletin de l'Agence Europe qui leur a accordé l'autorisation de reproduire ce texte.

La Cour tient à souligner qu'elle est entièrement en faveur du principe selon lequel de telles Conventions doivent lui attribuer des compétences appropriées, ceci en vue d'assurer tant l'unicité de la juridiction communautaire que l'application uniforme des Conventions dans tous les Etats membres. De l'avis de la Cour, l'augmentation du nombre des affaires qui résulterait de telles attributions supplémentaires ne devrait donc pas être une raison pour y renoncer, mais constitue en même temps un motif additionnel pour renforcer les effectifs et améliorer la structure de la Cour.

3. L'effet de ces trois facteurs — accroissement rapide du volume d'affaires; adhésion de nouveaux Etats membres; Conventions additionnelles — s'échelonne dans le temps.

A première vue, on pourrait dès lors estimer que seul le premier de ces facteurs exige des mesures immédiates, et c'est justement à ce titre que la Cour a déjà demandé la création d'un nouveau poste de référendaire pour chacun des cabinets de ses membres, demande dont elle tient à souligner encore l'extrême urgence.

La Cour est cependant d'avis qu'il convient d'ores et déjà d'envisager les trois éléments susmentionnés dans leur ensemble. En effet, dans l'élaboration de propositions tendant à remédier aux difficultés actuelles, on ne saurait raisonnablement faire abstraction d'événements futurs dont il est certain qu'ils soulèveront des problèmes analogues ou comparables. En outre, la Cour estime que c'est dans l'intérêt général de faire face à l'ensemble des exigences en question dans un esprit d'économie et de cohérence. Plus précisément, il convient d'éviter, dans la mesure du possible, qu'à plusieurs reprises au cours de quelques années, la Cour soit obligée, d'une part, de modifier radicalement son organisation et ses méthodes de travail et, d'autre part, de demander l'intervention du Conseil, voire des Etats membres.

4. Les demandes exposées au présent mémorandum visent pour la plupart des modifications ne nécessitant pas la mise en œuvre de la procédure de révision des traités, mais simplement des mesures à prendre par le Conseil en vertu des pouvoirs qu'il tient:

— soit des articles 165, alinéa 4, et 166, alinéa 3, du traité CEE et des dispositions correspondantes des autres traités (augmentation du nombre des juges et des avocats généraux; adaptation de certaines dispositions relatives à la structure de la Cour);
— soit de l'article 188, alinéa 2, du traité CEE et des dispositions correspondantes des autres traités (approbation de modifications du règlement de procédure établies par la Cour).

II. LES DEMANDES DE LA COUR.

Les demandes exposées ci-dessous s'inspirent de deux considérations fondamentales:

D'une part, la capacité de travail de tout juge et de tout avocat général n'étant pas illimitée, la Cour ne pourra, en fin de compte, maîtriser ses charges accrues de manière satisfaisante que si le nombre des magistrats est augmenté.

D'autre part, afin de pouvoir garantir un rendement optimal et maintenir la durée des procédures dans des limites raisonnables, il est nécessaire qu'au sein de la Cour, plusieurs formations juridictionnelles puissent siéger et délibérer en même temps et que cette simultanéité puisse jouer pour un grand nombre d'affaires. Dans un premier temps, il est proposé de constituer, au sein de la Cour, grâce à une augmentation modérée des effectifs, deux Chambres qui seraient en mesure d'assumer une proportion plus appréciable des affaires actuellement dévolues à la Cour plénière. Ainsi, la Cour plénière n'aurait à siéger plus que dans les affaires déterminées en fonction de leur importance particulière.

1. Mesures à prendre dans l'immédiat

A. *Enoncé des demandes*

a) Le nombre des juges devrait être porté à 12 et celui des avocats généraux à 6.

b) Jusqu'à l'adhésion de nouveaux Etats membres, la Cour en formation plénière continuerait à siéger au nombre de 9 juges, avec un quorum de 7. Ceci viserait à garder intact le caractère en même temps équilibré et pleinement représentatif que la Cour a actuellement.

c) La répartition des compétences entre la Cour plénière, d'une part, et les Chambres, d'autre part, serait modifiée de telle façon que la Cour plénière n'aurait désormais à connaître que des affaires soulevant des questions de droit revêtant une importance fondamentale pour la Communauté ou pour un ou plusieurs Etats membres. L'attribution des affaires relèverait de la décision autonome de la Cour, et ne serait donc plus rattachée à la qualité du requérant (cfr. article 165, alinéa 3 du Traité CEE) ou à la position adoptée, dans les affaires préjudicielles, par les Etats membres ou les institutions (cfr. article 95, paragraphe 1, alinéa 3 du règlement de procédure).

d) Les dispositions en vigueur seraient aménagées en ce sens que la Cour soit liée le moins possible quant au nombre et à la composition de ses Chambres ainsi qu'à la répartition des compétences entre les Chambres, en d'autres termes qu'elle puisse en décider en fonction de son travail et à la lumière de l'expérience sans avoir chaque fois à demander l'intervention du Conseil au titre d'une adaptation des traités ou de l'autorisation d'une modification du règlement de procédure.

e) L'article 9, paragraphe 2, alinéa 1 du règlement de procédure serait aménagé de telle façon que le Président de la Cour ne soit plus tenu de désigner l'avocat général, pour une affaire déterminée, au sein de la Chambre à laquelle cette affaire a été attribuée.

f) L'article 27, paragraphe 7, première phrase dudit règlement serait aménagé en ce sens que certaines décisions administratives puissent être prises par un corps restreint de magistrats (composé, par exemple, du Président de la Cour, des Présidents de Chambre, du Premier avocat général et d'un ou deux juges par Chambre).

B. *Motivation et explications*

a) Le dégagement de la Cour plénière en faveur des Chambres s'impose pour des raisons d'économie de travail.

1° En l'état actuel des textes, la Cour ne peut attribuer aux Chambres que les affaires de fonctionnaires et — dans les limites très étroites tracées par l'article 95, paragraphe 1, alinéas 1 et 3 — certaines affaires préjudicielles. Cette réglementation a conduit en pratique à ce que la grande majorité du total des affaires et la presque totalité des affaires préjudicielles doivent être retenues au niveau de la Cour plénière.

A la date du 30 juin 1978, par exemple, sur les 194 affaires dont la Cour était saisie, 171, soit 88,1 %, rentraient dans la compétence de la Cour plénière. Sur les 70 affaires préjudicielles en instance devant la Cour à cette date, 1, soit 1,3 % seulement, avait pu être renvoyée à une Chambre.

Or, un tel état de choses, non seulement diffère de la situation telle qu'elle existe auprès des juridictions suprêmes de tous les Etats membres, mais encore et surtout est de nature à diminuer considérablement le rendement de la Cour.

2° Il est évident que, plus le nombre des participants est grand, plus il est difficile d'organiser un délibéré utile, c'est-à-dire à la fois approfondi, expéditif et permettant à tout participant de faire valoir son point de vue. Aussi y a-t-il intérêt à limiter au maximum le nombre des affaires dans lesquelles l'organe judiciaire est obligé à délibérer dans une composition de plus de 7 membres.

b) Pour un autre motif encore, la capacité de rendement de la Cour se trouvera sensiblement renforcée si les présentes demandes sont accueillies.

Il est exact que, d'ores et déjà, les deux Chambres de la Cour, statuant chacune à 3 juges, sont en mesure de siéger et de délibérer simultanément. Mais cet avantage est de portée modeste, puisqu'aussi bien, la plupart des affaires sont traitées par le plénum, et il est par hypothèse exclu que celui-ci et une Chambre travaillent en même temps.

Cette situation pourra être améliorée à partir du moment où le total des effectifs permettra de former des Chambres comportant un nombre plus étendu de juges et, pour cette raison, plus représentatives que les Chambres actuelles. La simultanéité des travaux pourra jouer alors pour un nombre plus grand d'affaires.

c) S'il est loisible au Président de la Cour de désigner l'avocat général sans tenir compte de son appartenance à telle ou telle Chambre, la répartition des affaires entre les différents avocats généraux pourra se faire avec plus de souplesse, ce qui permettra mieux qu'à présent de veiller à l'égalité des charges.

2. Mesures à prendre en fonction de l'adhésion de la Grèce, du Portugal et de l'Espagne

a) Si les demandes de la Cour quant à l'augmentation immédiate du nombre des juges (de 9 à 12) et des avocats généraux (de 4 à 6) étaient admises, il serait à prévoir que, à la suite de l'adhésion, il faudrait procéder à une deuxième augmentation de ce nombre. Ce serait alors un pas dans la direction de la situation finale qui devrait être atteinte lorsque la Convention sur le brevet communautaire commencera à sortir son plein effet. Le nombre des avocats généraux devrait, en principe, correspondre à la moitié de celui des juges.

b) L'adhésion des trois Etats-candidats comportera, de toute façon, une révision des traités. La Cour est d'avis qu'on pourrait saisir cette occasion pour essayer de résoudre un problème dont elle souligne la grande importance:

A l'heure actuelle, la Cour statue en premier et dernier ressort dans toutes les catégories d'affaires. En matière de contentieux des agents, des travaux sont déjà en cours en vue de la création d'un tribunal administratif de première instance contre les décisions duquel un recours en révision pourra être introduit devant la Cour qui ainsi ne statuera plus que sur des points de droit. La Cour souligne l'urgence de l'achèvement de ces travaux.

La Cour admet qu'il paraît opportun de maintenir la situation actuelle en ce qui concerne, notamment, des catégories d'affaires telles que les recours en manquement d'Etat, les recours en annulation intentés par les Etats membres ou les institutions communautaires et — en tout cas — les affaires préjudicielles. En revanche, il est permis de se demander si certaines autres catégories d'affaires — tels les recours introduits par les particuliers en matière de concurrence (articles 85 et 86 du Traité CEE) ou de responsabilité (articles 178, 215 de ce traité) — ne pourraient pas à l'avenir faire l'objet d'une réglementation analogue à celle qui est actuellement envisagée pour le contentieux des agents.

Il convient de faire observer que, contrairement à ce qui vaut pour le contentieux des agents, une mesure de ce genre ne pourrait pas être prise par simple voie réglementaire. En effet, une disposition comparable à celle de l'article 179 du Traité CEE — aux termes de laquelle la Cour n'est compétente pour statuer sur ledit contentieux que « dans les limites et conditions déterminées au statut ou résultant du régime applicable [aux agents] » — fait défaut aux autres articles attribuant des compétences à la Cour.

Une telle réforme aurait l'avantage non seulement de rapprocher le système judiciaire de la Communauté de celui de tous les Etats membres, mais encore et surtout de conférer à la Cour, dans une large mesure, la fonction de juge du droit à l'exclusion de celle de juge du fait, ce qui accentuerait davantage la véritable et principale mission qui revient à la Cour au sein de la Communauté. Le rôle de la Cour se limiterait ainsi à statuer sur les recours en cassation ou en révision qui seraient intentés devant elle contre les décisions de la nouvelle juridiction de première instance.

Sur le plan structurel et administratif, cette juridiction devrait être organiquement liée à la Cour elle-même.

Si le Conseil devait estimer que le besoin de créer une telle instance ne sera pas urgent même au moment de l'adhésion, il serait de toute façon utile de modifier le texte des traités en ce sens qu'une telle création n'exigerait désormais que l'intervention du Conseil.

3. Mesures à prendre en fonction des nouvelles compétences de la Cour résultant de l'entrée en vigueur de certaines conventions, et notamment de la Convention sur le brevet communautaire

Ainsi qu'il a été dit plus haut, la Cour part de la présomption selon laquelle ce sera à partir de 1984 environ qu'elle subira la plénitude des charges que lui imposera la Convention sur le brevet communautaire. Compte tenu de l'ampleur prévisible de ces charges, elle estime que, dès 1984, elle devra être composée de 17 juges et d'un nombre approprié d'avocats généraux qui, en principe, devrait correspondre à la moitié du nombre des juges.

Il serait prématuré de présenter dès maintenant des propositions concrètes quant à la structure (nombre, composition et compétence des Chambres, etc.) que la Cour devrait avoir à cette époque-là. Toutefois, dans ce contexte, la Cour tient à rappeler sa demande exposée plus haut et tendant à ce que les dispositions relatives à la structure de la Cour soient dès à présent assouplies, de manière à permettre désormais à la Cour, dans toute la mesure du possible, de modifier son organisation, en fonction de son travail et à la lumière de l'expérience, sans avoir à demander l'autorisation du Conseil. Par exemple, une Cour composée de 17 juges disposerait de possibilités variées quant à la formation de Chambres.

Annexe au mémorandum de la Cour : Données statistiques

Nombre des affaires introduites

1957:	19	Ces chiffres se rapportent chaque fois à l'année entière
1967:	37	
1974:	110	
1975:	135	
1976:	132	
1977:	164	
1978 (six premiers mois)	156	

On peut signaler en outre que, du 1er janvier au 30 juin 1978, le nombre des affaires pendantes devant la Cour a augmenté de 132 à 194.

Dans cette statistique, chacune des affaires ayant ultérieurement fait l'objet d'une jonction a été comptée séparément.

Nombre des arrêts rendus

1974:	62	Ces chiffres se rapportent chaque fois à l'année entière
1975:	78	
1976:	88	
1977:	100	
1978 (six premiers mois)	60	

Les arrêts rendus dans des affaires jointes ont été comptés chaque fois comme un seul arrêt.

Il convient d'ailleurs de faire observer que le degré croissant de difficulté et de complexité que revêt la moyenne des affaires portées devant la Cour ajoute encore considérablement au fardeau que celle-ci doit supporter.

B. FONCTIONNEMENT DE LA COUR DE JUSTICE

Sur la base d'un mémorandum de la Cour de Justice, relatif aux mesures qu'elle juge nécessaires aux fins de son fonctionnement actuel et futur, le Conseil a procédé à un échange de vues à l'issue duquel il a marqué son accord sur la déclaration suivante:

« LE CONSEIL DES COMMUNAUTES EUROPEENNES,

— ayant pris connaissance du mémorandum de la Cour sur les mesures qu'elle juge nécessaires aux fins de son fonctionnement actuel et futur, partage le souci de celle-ci de maintenir la qualité et le rendement du travail juridictionnel;

— confirme sa volonté ferme de prendre les mesures qui seraient dans son pouvoir pour permettre à la Cour de continuer, vu l'augmentation considérable de la charge du travail de cette institution, à accomplir de manière consciencieuse et rapide la mission que lui ont confiée les traités;

— exprime une opinion favorable à une adaptation des règles de procédure qui, dans le respect des principes fondamentaux de la procédure et de l'organisation judiciaire, permette d'assurer des conditions de fonctionnement optimales de la Cour et de maintenir la durée des procédures dans les limites raisonnables;

— prend acte des suggestions de la Cour d'augmenter le nombre des juges et des avocats généraux;

— charge le Comité des Représentants Permanents de faire examiner dans les meilleurs délais l'ensemble des propositions que la Cour pourrait présenter à la lumière des délibérations de ce jour, et de faire un premier rapport dans un délai de 6 mois après leur présentation. »

C. TRIBUNAL POUR LITIGES ENTRE LES INSTITUTIONS ET LEUR PERSONNEL

Le Conseil,

ayant pris acte de la proposition de la Commission, du 4 août 1978, de règlement visant à modifier le statut des fonctionnaires et à créer un Tribunal Administratif des Communautés Européennes, ainsi que de l'opinion exprimée par la Cour dans sa lettre du 22 juillet 1974, selon laquelle la création de ce tribunal peut s'effectuer par voie de modification du statut des fonctionnaires;

considérant qu'une décision relative à cette proposition ne pourra être arrêtée que lorsque les avis de l'Assemblée et de la Cour de Justice seront connus;

se référant à sa décision du 26 novembre 1974, dans laquelle il a donné son accord de principe sur l'opportunité de la création d'une juridiction de première instance;

convenant de prévoir une première instance qui statue tant en droit qu'en fait sur les litiges opposant les membres du personnel et l'autorité investie du pouvoir de nomination, en réservant à la Cour la compétence de statuer en dernier ressort sur toutes les questions de droit;

— demande au Comité des Représentants Permanents de faire engager les délibérations sur cette proposition dès réception des avis précités, et de faire en sorte que les travaux soient conclus si possible dans un délai de neuf mois.

(...)

II. — LE MEMORANDUM BRITANNIQUE

THE BRITISH SUGGESTIONS CONCERNING THE COURT OF JUSTICE *

(Editorial Comments extraits de *Common Market Law Review,* février 1979, pp. 3 à 7)

At its 537th session the Council of Ministers, composed of the Ministers of Justice, discussed a memorandum of the British Government to improve the participation of Member States in cases before the Court. In that memorandum the British Government stressed the importance of the judgments of the Court on two grounds: First, the judgments cover matters which are of great interest to the Member States, which govern their mutual relations and which are usually of national government concern. Secondly, in most cases the texts on which the Court rules cannot be easily changed. When a national supreme court gives an objectionable judgment, the legislature can overrule it by changing the relevant laws. In the Communities this is far more difficult. According to the British Government the Member States should be more closely involved in the Court's proceedings. For this purpose four suggestions were made:

(1) In the case of references under Article 177 the period of two months which is granted to Member States to make their observations should be extended. This period is too short for the necessary legal research and consultation between government departments.

(2) National courts do not always clearly formulate their questions when they request preliminary rulings. Therefore Member States may find it difficult to decide whether they should submit observations and, if so, on what issues. It would therefore be helpful if the Court of Justice would identify the real issues for decision at an early stage of the proceedings, preferably before the opportunity for written observations is closed and certainly before the oral stage.

(3) In preliminary proceedings the parties and the Member States have insufficient opportunity to contest each others' arguments. Before the Court of Justice the written, rather than the oral proceedings carry the greater weight, partly because of translation problems in the oral proceedings, partly because of the tradition of the Court. As all the written comments must be presented at the same time, the Member States have no opportunity to meet in their written submissions the arguments advanced by the parties, the Commission or by other Member States. Such an opportunity should be granted.

(4) In direct actions of individuals against Community Institutions the Governments may intervene, but that must be done in a formal way under Article 93 of the Rules of Procedure. And then one of the two parties must be supported. Member States should have a more adequate opportunity to present observations. They should have access to the pleadings in order to be able to decide whether to intervene and on what arguments. They should not be required to support either of the parties.

In the same session the Council of Ministers discussed measures to be taken in order to cope with the problems caused by the steady increase of cases brought before the Court of Justice. The number of 19 in 1957 rose to 37 in 1967, to 164 in 1977 and to 268 (of which 100 were joined cases) in 1978. The time is long past when a bottle of champagne could be opened when a new case was brought before the Court. The discussion was initiated by a memorandum of the Court itself. The Council agreed to several measures, such as the appointment of a second legal secretary to every judge and the creation of a special tribunal for staff cases. But it did not agree to an increase in the number of judges. During these debates the British delegation made a fifth suggestion:

---

* NDLR : les organisateurs de la journée d'études remercient la rédaction de la *Common Market Law Review* qui leur a accordé l'autorisation de reproduire ce texte.

(5) In the opinion of the British Government the work-load of the Court could be eased by bringing less cases before it. When the Community is extended to twelve Members there will be all the more reason to revise the tasks as originally given to a Court for six States. An important reduction in the number of cases could be achieved by providing that preliminary rulings should only be requested in cases of great general importance. The Government probably wanted to return to an old British suggestion to restrict the right of requesting preliminary rulings to appellate courts.

The British suggestions have raised considerable opposition, in particular in the Netherlands. The leading newspaper *NRC Handelsblad* spoke of a "political attack on the Court" (issue of 10 October). In its leading article the same newspaper wrote more fatalistically that this was bound to happen. Now that the supranational forces in Europe have been lamed an attack had to come on the only institution which still supports the original conception of European Integration. One could not expect that integration would go on indefinitely in the legal field while in other fields opposition continuously grows. According to the Dutch newspapers the Netherlands' Minister of Justice was entirely right in force fully objecting to the British proposals.

It seems unlikely that the British proposals are meant as an attack on the Court. They are probably intended to improve the functioning of the Court through better participation of the Member States. Nonetheless the spirit of the proposals to some extent justifies fervent Dutch reactions. According to a large part of Dutch public opinion the Communities are — or at least should be — supranational institutions which independently look after the interests of the citizens. In a way they constitute a safeguard against the ever increasing powers of the national governments. They may help by giving some counterweight against those governments. When the Dutch authorities charged too much, van Gend and Loos could successfully invoke Community Law against them. Since them many other Dutchmen have used Community Law against their own Government. The British proposals, on the other hand, breathe the spirit of a close linkage between the Community and the national governments. In the British view the Community is not a new supranational authority but only a means for cooperation between national governments. In such a Community the national authorities should be heard as much as possible and should play a maximum role, also in Court proceedings. It is probably this general attitude more than the individual proposals which raised opposition.

Nonetheless the individual suggestions as well merit some comment.

(1) A time-limit of two months for comments on preliminary questions is very short indeed. But, on the other hand, the preliminary ruling is an interim measure in national court proceedings which necessarily causes unwanted delay. That delay should be as brief as possible. For the parties to the dispute, who have pleaded before the national court and who know the case, two months is sufficient. Most Member States have succeeded in organising their internal proceedings in such a way that comments can be given in time. Under pressure of time the British Government might be able to do the same. If not, a small extension would probably not cause great harm.

(2) The second suggestion causes more problems. Usually the Court will be able to discern clearly the questions involved only after it has received the written observations from the parties, the Commission and sometimes from Member States. If after that the Member States were to get a new opportunity to make written comments, this would indeed cause considerable delay. There are only very few cases in which the Court of Justice finally rules on a question which has hot been clearly asked by the national court concerned. An example may be the *Simmenthal* case (Case 70/77 of 28 June 1978, (1978) E.C.R. 1453, considerations 57-68) in which the Court rules on Directives 64/433 and 64/432, though no question on those directives had been asked. Such cases are exceptional, however, and it may be doubted whether comments of Member Governments would be of sufficient importance to warrant a considerable delay. Perhaps it would be possible to allow the Court to give an interim ruling in which to state that further comments will be needed on affiliated questions and to grant the Member States and the Commission an additional time-limit of one or two months to provide such information. The Court should then be free to judge whether an extension

of the time needed for the preliminary ruling is justified. It would be still easier to leave the problem to the Court itself. It will usually recognise the problem and of its own motion ask the Member States for their comments, as it did in, *e.g.*, the *De Bloos* case (14/76 of 6 October 1976, (1976) E.C.R. 1501).

(3) In its third suggestion the British Government touches on a serious problem. Frequently preliminary rulings are asked for on the question whether Community Law permits a particular kind of national legislation. In fact these are questions on the legality of such national legislation. The parties in the dispute have ample opportunity to exchange arguments for and against such legality before their national court. For them it is sufficient to have one written and one oral opportunity to make observations to the Court of Justice. But for the Member State concerned the legality of its own legislation may be of the greatest importance, and it may not be involved at all in the domestic litigation. In the *Laughing Dolls* case (22/76 of 22 September 1976, (1976) E.C.R. 1371) a French importer sued an Italian exporter before an Italian court for payment of an import fine charged by the French authorities. The preliminary ruling asked for by the Italian court was of the greatest importance to the legality of the French import fine. The French Government received the case from the Court of Justice and had to prepare its defence within two months without having seen the argument of the Commission which considered the import fine to be illegal. In such cases better opportunities for the State concerned seem to be required. The Court of Justice is aware of this problem and indicated a possible solution in one of the *Simmenthal cases* when it held that it may "prove to be in the interest of the proper administration of justice that a question should be referred for a preliminary ruling only after both sides have been heard" (Case 70/77 of 28 June 1978, (1978) E.C.R. 1453, consideration 10). This may be seen as an invitation to the national judiciaries to allow or, when they have such power, to invite the national authorities to intervene in cases where the legality of national acts is at stake. This is not always possible, nor may it be enough. It would, therefore, be proper to allow States whose national legislation is involved in preliminary questions to send in a second set of written comments within one month after the observations of the Commission and of the parties have been received.

(4) In their fourth suggestion the British Government clearly demonstrate their wish to see the Community as an inter-governmental activity. Others may wish to grant a similar right of access to the pleadings to the European Parliament. The suggestion has little merit. When individuals come directly to the Court of Justice they either challenge the validity of a Community act or they sue for damages. In neither of those cases is there much room for a position different from that of the parties, such as wished by the Government. When an act of the Council is at stake the Governments know perfectly well what is involved and do not need access to the pleadings. When an act of the Commission is involved the pleadings may contain information, *e.g.* on the capacity of an undertaking to pay fines, which the parties do not want to reveal to their Governments and which the Governments do not need.

(5) Finally the British suggestion to limit the cases in which preliminary rulings can be requested. It may be appropriate to urge national courts to ask for preliminary rulings only in cases where they are really needed; it would be wrong to limit the right of requesting preliminary rulings to appellate courts. Over thirty preliminary rulings have been requested on the classification for the common customs tariff on products such as bulk caramel, chrome tanned skins, mechanically propelled locomotives, potteries, ice cream, mining machinery, imitation lard, artistic screen prints, children's picture books and copying paper. As far as the customs tariff is concerned, uniformity throughout the Community is essential. It may be that in Britain such questions are solved by the customs authorities which may consult the administration in Brussels, but in other Member States individuals may challenge the opinion of the customs authorities before a court and that court must decide. It would be an unacceptable burden on the parties to force them to bring an appeal before an appellate court in cases where the substantial decision is taken by the Court of Justice and where, therefore, the national court decision can equally well be taken at first instance.

Although some points in the British memorandum can lead to important improvements other points may need some further consideration. The Ministers of Justice have referred the Memorandum to the Committee of Permanent Representatives.

LISTE DES INTERVENANTS

PAULIN, B., conseiller au service juridique de la Commission des Communautés européennes, Bruxelles, pp. 27, 58-59.

PESCATORE, P., juge à la Cour de justice des Communautés européennes, Luxembourg, pp. 27-28, 28, 54-55.

PUISSOCHET, J.-P., directeur des affaires juridiques de l'OCDE, Paris (France), p. 51.

RASMUSSEN, Hjalte, Associate Professor of Law, Copenhagen Business School, Institute for European Market Law, Copenhague (Danemark), pp. 58, 90.

RYZIGER, P.-Fr., avocat au Conseil d'Etat et à la Cour de cassation, Paris (France), pp. 56-57, 85-86, 88.

WAELBROECK, M., professeur à la Faculté de droit de l'Université libre de Bruxelles, p. 29.

LISTE DES ABREVIATIONS COURANTES

AFDI	Annuaire français de droit international
AJDA	Actualité juridique. Droit administratif
Bull. CE	Bulletin des Communautés européennes
Cah.dr.eur.	Cahiers de droit européen
CECA	Communauté européenne du charbon et de l'acier
CEE	Communauté économique européenne
CEEA	Communauté européenne de l'énergie atomique
Clunet	Journal de droit international
CML Rev.	Common Market Law Review
D	Recueil Dalloz
EuGRZ	Europaïsche - Grundrechte Zeitschrift
JCP	Jurisclasseur périodique. La semaine juridique
JOCE	Journal officiel des Communautés européennes
RCADI	Recueil des cours de l'Académie de droit international, La Haye
Rec.	Recueil de la jurisprudence de la Cour de justice des Communautés européennes
RMC	Revue du Marché commun
Rev. trim. dr. com.	Revue trimestrielle de droit commercial
Rev. trim. dr. eur.	Revue trimestrielle de droit européen.

TABLE DES MATIERES

BIBLIOTHÈQUE
DE L'INSTITUT D'ÉTUDES EUROPÉENNES
(EXTRAIT DU COLLOQUE)

COLLOQUES EUROPEENS

* **Les Droits de l'Homme en droit interne et en droit international.** Actes du deuxième colloque international sur la Convention européenne des Droits de l'Homme, Vienne, 18-20 octobre 1965, relié, 1968, 593 pages. 765 FB

* **La décision dans les Communautés européennes.** Actes du colloque de l'Association pour le développement de la science politique européenne, Lyon, 11 et 12 novembre 1966, relié, 1969, XXIV + 511 pages. 840 FB

* **Les institutions juridiques du gouvernement de l'économie dans les pays occidentaux et socialistes.** Colloque, Bruxelles, 23-26 mai 1966, relié, 1968, 419 pages. 585 FB

* **Vers une politique industrielle européenne.** Colloque, Bruxelles, 24 et 25 octobre 1968, 1970, IX + 339 pages. 720 FB

* **Droit pénal européen — Europees strafrecht — European Criminal Law.** Congrès, Bruxelles, 7-9 novembre 1968, 1970, XIII + 665 pages. 980 FB

* **Les régions frontalières à l'heure du Marché commun.** Colloque, Bruxelles, 27 et 28 novembre 1969, 1970, XIII + 427 pages, 12 planches en couleur hors texte. 780 FB

* **La Commission des Communautés européennes et l'élargissement de l'Europe.** Colloque, Bruxelles, 23-25 novembre 1972, 1974, XI + 340 pages. 690 FB

* **La crise de l'emploi. Diagnostic et examen de quelques solutions. — Employment Crisis, Diagnostic and Possible Solutions.** Journée d'études, 2 décembre 1975, brochure ronéotée, 1976, 174 pages. 325 FB

* **Les relations du Maroc et de la Communauté économique européenne.** Journées d'études, 24 et 25 mai 1976, brochure ronéotée, 1977, 164 pages. 270 FB

* **La Grèce et la Communauté. Problèmes posés par l'adhésion.** Colloque, Bruxelles, 5 et 6 mai 1977, 1978, 352 pages. 595 FB

* **Le rôle de l'Europe dans le nouvel ordre économique international.** Colloque, Bruxelles, 13-14 octobre 1978, 1979, 356 pages. 690 FB

* **L'Espagne et les Communautés européennes. Problèmes posés par l'adhésion.** Colloque organisé conjointement avec le Centre d'Etudes européennes et la Faculté de droit de l'Université catholique de Louvain, Louvain-la-Neuve, 25-26 mai 1979, 1979, 431 pages. 900 FB

LE DROIT DE LA COMMUNAUTE ECONOMIQUE EUROPEENNE

* Commentaire du traité et des textes pris pour son application, par J. MEGRET, M. WAELBROECK, J.-V. LOUIS, D. VIGNES et J.-L. DEWOST.

Vol. 1. **Préambule. Principes. Libre circulation des marchandises,** 1970, 336 pages (2e tirage) 500 FB

Vol. 2. **Agriculture,** 1970, 720 pages (2e tirage) 1100 FB

Vol. 3. **Libre circulation des travailleurs. Etablissement et services. Capitaux. Transports,** 1971, 584 pages (2e tirage) 820 FB

Vol. 4. **Concurrence,** 1972, 532 pages (2e tirage) 780 FB

Vol. 5. **Dispositions fiscales. Rapprochement des législations,** 1973, 390 pages 850 FB

Vol. 6. **Politique économique,** 2 tomes, 1976, 722 pages 1850 FB

Vol. 7. **Politique sociale,** 1973, 214 pages 495 FB

Vol. 8. **Banque européenne d'investissement,** 1979, 138 pages 450 FB

Vol. 9. **L'Assemblée. Le Conseil. La Commission. Le Comité économique et social,** 1979, 480 pages 1450 FB

Vol. 10. **La Cour de justice. Les actes des institutions** En préparation

Vol. 11. **Les dispositions financières** En préparation

Vol. 12. **Les relations extérieures** Sous presse

Vol. 13. **L'aide au développement** En préparation

Vol. 14. **Dispositions générales et finales** En préparation

THESES ET TRAVAUX JURIDIQUES

* **Brevets et marques au regard du droit de la concurrence en Europe et aux Etats-Unis,** Colloque, Bruxelles, les 15 et 16 novembre 1966, 1968, XII + 225 pages. 320 FB

* J.-V. LOUIS, **Les règlements de la Communauté économique européenne,** relié, 1969, XXXI + 517 pages. 980 FB

* **L'association à la Communauté économique européenne. Aspects juridiques,** 1970, XIV + 369 pages. 600 FB

* **Le régime juridique des titres de sociétés en Europe et aux Etats-Unis — The Legal Status of Securities in Europe and the United States,** relié, 1970,XXXII + 639 pages. 1280 FB

* **Les émissions de titres de sociétés en Europe et aux Etats-Unis — Corporate Securities Markets in Europe and the United States,** Colloque, Bruxelles, du 21 au 23 novembre 1968, 1970, XVIII + 412 pages. 980 FB

* C.O. Kim, **La Communauté économique européenne dans les relations commerciales internationales,** 1971, XI + 459 pages. 550 FB

* J. Velu, **L'affaire Delcourt. L'arrêt rendu le 17 janvier 1970 par la Cour européenne des droits de l'homme,** 1972, 78 pages. 270 FB

* P. Mertens, **Le droit de recours effectif devant les instances nationales en cas de violation d'un droit de l'homme,** 1973, XI + 161 pages. 480 FB

* M. Waelbroeck, **Les réglementations nationales de prix et le droit communautaire,** 1975, 64 pages. 140 FB

* D. de Ripainsel-Landy, A. Gerard, A. Limpens-Meinertzhagen, J.-V. Louis, P. Soldatos, R. Vander Elst, G. Vandersanden, **Les instruments du rapprochement des législations dans la Communauté économique européenne,** 1976, X + 195 pages. 560 FB

* **La Charte sociale européenne. Dix années d'application.** Colloque, Bruxelles, 14 et 15 octobre 1976, 1978, 336 pages. 640 FB

* C. Flaesch-Mougin, **Les accords externes de la Communauté économique européenne. Essai d'une typologie,** 1979, 320 pages. 750 FB

THESES ET TRAVAUX ECONOMIQUES

* L. Morissens, **La politique économique de la Communauté économique européenne,** 1965, 34 pages. Epuisé

* P. Romus, **La Wallonie dans la Communauté européenne,** 1967, 44 pages Epuisé

* M. Lisein-Norman, **L'évolution de l'aide de l'Europe aux pays sous-développés,** 1968, 46 pages Epuisé

* L. Morissens, **La cohérence de l'intégration des politiques économiques dans la Communauté économique européenne,** 1968, 82 pages Epuisé

* M. Lisein-Norman, **Le transfert des objectifs de politique économique des gouvernements nationaux à des autorités communautaires,** 1968, 51 pages 50 FB

* P. Kestens, **Prévisions des importations des pays développés capitalistes en provenance du monde sous-développé,** 1969, XIV + 239 pages 520 FB

* J. POELMANS et J. LECOMTE, **L'agriculture européenne et les pays tiers,** 1972, X + 185 pages 450 FB
* C. DELEPIERE-NYS, **Air-Europe. La politique de coopération entre les compagnies aériennes de l'Europe des Six,** 1974, XXXIX + 470 pages 780 FB
* M. LISEIN-NORMAN, **Les prestations familiales dans l'Europe des Six,** 1974, XXXIX + 419 pages 550 FB

THESES ET TRAVAUX POLITIQUES

* L. DIERICKX, **Het Europese Besluitvormingsproces en het Europese integratieproces : De totstandkoming van verordening nr 17,** 1972, 328 pages 680 FB
* D. PAULUS, **Les milieux dirigeants belges et l'adhésion du Royaume-Uni aux Communautés européennes,** 1971, 331 pages 594 FB
* N. BERNARD, C. LAVAL et A. NYS, **Le Comité économique et social,** 1972, XVIII + 283 pages 350 FB
* J. MEYNAUD et D. SIDJANSKI, **Les groupes de pression dans la Communauté européenne (1958-1968),** 1971, 733 pages 1170 FB
* P. SOLDATOS, **Les données fondamentales de la politique britannique à l'égard de la Communauté économique européenne (1955-1970),** 1973, XVIII + 195 pages 560 FB

CHRONOLOGIE DES COMMUNAUTES EUROPEENNES

* Volume 1 : **Les faits et les décisions de la Communauté économique européenne : 1958-1964,** par H. DORSCH et H. LEGROS, 1969, XVI + 543 pages 520 FB
* Volume 2 : **Les faits et les décisions de la Communauté économique européenne : 1965-1968,** par H. DORSCH et H. LEGROS, 1973, 901 pages 1495 FB
* Volume 3 : **Les faits et les décisions de la Communauté économique européennes : 1969,** par H. DORSCH, 1978, 320 pages 975 FB
* Volume 4 : **L'Union économique et monétaire : 1970-1973,** par H. DORSCH, J.-V. LOUIS et M. MICHIELS, 1977, 284 pages 680 FB

VARIA

* M. LISEIN-NORMAN, **La Suède face à l'intégration européenne,** brochure ronéotée, 1975, 131 pages 230 FB
* P. BOUVIER, **L'Europe et la coopération au développement. Un bilan : la convention de Lomé,** 1980, 191 pages 450 FB